THEORY
AND PRACTICE
AS A SINGLE REALITY

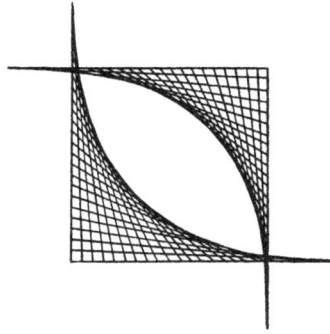

THEORY

AND PRACTICE

AS A SINGLE REALITY

An Essay in Social Work Education

by

RUTH GILPIN

CHAPEL HILL
THE UNIVERSITY OF NORTH CAROLINA PRESS

PRINTED BY THE SEEMAN PRINTERY, DURHAM, N.C.

ACKNOWLEDGMENTS

This book, an essay in social work education, is itself an acknowledgment of my own social work education. People of the past and present, known to me or unknown, possessing a viewpoint like that which has become mine or possessing a different one, have contributed to my education and to this book. Particularly, I would like to express my gratitude to my teachers Virginia P. Robinson and Anita J. Faatz, who with Jessie Taft, the "single reality" of my beginning as a student of social work, have their special places in what I write and what I hope I give to students of my own. There are others, too, who have been important to me in this educational endeavor: my present colleagues, Arthur E. Fink and Isabelle K. Carter of the University of North Carolina School of Social Work; the faculty there with whom I share daily the problems and the rewards of teaching social work students; my advisers and colleagues of the past at the University of Pennsylvania School of Social Work, Ruth E. Smalley, Margaret E. Bishop, and Harold Lewis. To these faculty members of two schools, I express my appreciation.

But how can I properly express appreciation to the

many students, their supervisors, and their field work agencies who appear anonymously in these pages or who do not appear at all and yet are present? I simply say thank you to them all and to Christine Bowman, who has typed and re-typed the manuscript with unfailing willingness and skill.

Chapel Hill
February, 1963

CONTENTS

PART ONE

THE PROBLEM OF DUALITY

1

INTRODUCTION

This is an essay on teaching and learning. Its theme is one that through years of practice in casework and supervision and teaching of social work I have come back to again and again. It appears to me now as the uniting of practice and theory into a single reality, whereas earlier in my experience it appeared either as the assumption of responsibility for the supervision of a foster home, for example, or as the nature of yielding as the core of the helping process. The inner creative impulse, I believe, goes persistently in its own direction through the years, accompanied by the will to carry the impulse out, the emotion to sustain it, and the intellect to give it stature—all as one in the one person who can know his direction as no one else can. So it has been that this topic, always exciting and ever new to me, is truly personally chosen.

An essay in this day of science may seem anachronistic to those educators who like many other professional people are seeking precision in method and knowledge and definition. An essay is one person's attempt or trial to express and develop a particular theme that touches both the feelings and the intellect of the reader as well as those of the essayist himself.

Were this book presented as formal research, however, the element of personal interest could not be eliminated. Barzun and Graff recognize that it is both impossible and undesirable to do so.[1] Any point of view taken in relation to past events, which include yesterday's, comes from the individual writer's or researcher's present moment and immediate concern. One danger to research may lie more in the avowal that personal interest does not exist and does not affect the research than in the avowal that personal interest cannot be eliminated. The choice from which evolves form, topic and problem, content, point of view, method and arrangement in thesis or essay comes from the individual's own self, the self that has made prior choices for its own nurture and expression. Personal interest is the wellspring of any work's creation.

The content of this essay, then, will have to do with practice and theory and the uniting of the two, especially in the field of education for social work. The basic problem underlying this content and its development is a pedagogical one of concern to teachers in schools of social work and to the supervisors of the school's students having their field practice in the social agencies.

The human being who cannot move or conceive of moving in two directions at one time must, when he chooses, choose singly. If this is so, as we assume here, then the human being who is a student of a professional school might never unite his theory with his practice, for no matter how short the time interval between class work and field practice, a gap would always remain which he could not close. The pedagogical problem, it seems, is that of how to present the student with a program the single nature of

1. Jacques Barzun and Henry F. Graff, *The Modern Researcher* (New York: Harcourt, Brace and Company, 1957), pp. 53-54.

which he can choose in order to learn and to integrate his learning. In other words, the problem becomes one of bringing together the two distinct parts of the educational structure, professional school and practice agency.

In this problem we face the age-old question of the philosophic "analytic-synthetic" debate, the psychological "knowledge-experience," the professional "theory-practice." For all the centuries of debating, the question still remains: can they be made one? The logical answer is no. For many educators and social workers for whom the logical answer is indeed no, the empirical answer is yes. They find in experience that the two parts do somehow come together, and the student learns or the client is helped. The nature of this coming together is the concern of this essay; in it I shall suggest a clue to the resolution of the problem, but I shall not end or pretend to end the debate.

The meanings of the terms "theory" and "practice" are not so simple and clear-cut as they often seem. All educators and all those who have been to school would agree that within the context of teaching and learning are many diverse elements in both classroom and practice agency. It is no less than amazing when we stop to think of it that pupils learn at all; yet they do. Six professors with six different subjects and six different personalities, and six different viewpoints; a supervisor in the agency with yet another area of instruction, another personality, another point from which he views the field; and the lone student is expected to integrate this variety! More than that, he is expected to learn first in one setting and then in another, for the school on campus may be separated by miles or hundreds of miles from the practice agency. Withal, the student does learn and does become a social worker with a beginning competence, not yet a skill, in a method of helping which, for this essay, will be that of social casework.

How this learning comes about can be accounted for by way of various theories and through the operation of various educational structures. There may be actually as many different educational schemes in existence among the schools of social work as there are schools—and as many schemes for improving education by ironing out the diversities or by deepening the understanding of the human nature in teaching and learning. The accrediting body for the schools of social work (the Council on Social Work Education) has as one of its aims the bringing about of a base of uniformity and at the same time acknowledging that each school may and must maintain its own right to develop creatively and its own urge to possess integrity. A judgment as to which theory is best, or which structure, has never been successfully made, and it may be that making such a judgment fortunately is impossible. In the youth of any profession such as social work in this age—or perhaps of any profession in any age—its very life may depend upon the ability of its member schools to accept and to act out of their own differences.

In this book, a certain point of view will be frankly admitted and presented. It seems perhaps even more accurate to say that in this book a certain "generative principle" prevails. The term "generative principle" was originated and analyzed in detail by Paul Schrecker,[2] and it expresses what is meant here better than do "school of thought" and "guide to action," although it includes both. Simply stated, a generative principle is a principle that, through the work of those who choose it, generates exploration leading to the uncovering of subsidiary principles. These principles in turn require of the social worker (or scientist or artist or statesman) further work and finer performance. Consequently, the generative principle becomes life-giving through human

2. Paul Schrecker, *Work and History: An Essay on Civilization* (Princeton: Princeton University Press, 1948).

work. It stays alive even when no one chooses it or works at it, as long as there are questions about it as yet unanswered or paradoxes within it as yet unresolved. But to grow and to generate and to uncover the as yet unseen, this principle must be carried out by human work. Through human work, a generative principle can become, over time, a scientific experiment on a grand scale.

Such a principle I chose many years ago. In social work its name is *functional,* whether the work be that of teaching or supervising or helping troubled people who are clients of a social agency. The functional generative principle is chosen by a minority of professional social workers.

Arising from this principle are both an unresolved paradox and the possible resolution. That the nature of human choice is single has been a major contribution of functional social work education; and yet the schools of social work, including those teaching functional social work, offer a diversity, a multiplicity of reality choices within their programs. The resolution of the paradox through reduction of that multiplicity to a single reality will be the theme of this book.

In developing this theme, there will be first a brief review of the literature of the past with its indication of the nature of the practice-theory problem and the early efforts to solve it. This review will indicate, too, the discovery of casework principles and the erection of educational structures by which these principles could be transmitted to others. From the beginning of professional social work education, class work in the school has been alternated with field practice in the agency. On one plan, named "Concurrent," this alternation is by days in the week; on the other plan, named "Block," the alternation is by school terms of weeks or months. On either plan, a gap between practice and theory remains and the student's reality choices are multiple.

Next, moving to more recent years and what might be

called the present, further discussion of the theory from which the theme of this essay arises will entail reference to other theories of education and other modes of educational practice. Our belief that man's single nature and single choice requires a single external reality in order to find his own truth stems from the functional generative principle. This belief, or theory, will be differentiated from or likened to other theories and principles in order to clarify it for those who practice within it and those who do not. The acceptance of difference in others which we social workers claim with pride is more difficult to achieve than we often want to believe, for it asks of us first to accept our own difference, to be who we are, to maintain our own identity, in the face even of majority trends or forces.

The School of Social Work of the University of North Carolina has willingly opened its files, so to speak, with the permission of supervisors and students. This school's practice will be described in some detail in order to observe how one school endeavors to achieve a concurrence with the field work agency and then to assume for itself a fusion of school-agency as the single reality for the student to choose. This school's operation on the Block Plan, an operation still unfinished and growing, is presented not as the only way for a school and an agency to reach concurrence and fusion, but *one* way.

As far as this particular school is concerned, it is neither finished nor perfect but, for the frozen moment of this writing, an admission of fulfillment is readily professed. Fulfillment that is momentary in nature at once breaks up as the creative individual or school begins immediately to work on the mistakes, on what has been left undone, on what is as yet unseen, on moving toward fuller life and growth.

The University of North Carolina school's basic structure is Block. Roughly speaking, only about one-fifth of the sixty-three schools of social work operate under this plan. There was a time, as we shall see, when almost all social workers looked with deep distrust upon a plan whereby class and field alternated by months of time and were separated spatially by hundreds of miles. This plan is no longer a poor substitute for the Concurrent Plan; it is a self-respecting and effective structure for social work education. It will continue to be needed wherever local field placements are insufficient.

A question that is directly connected with what is being attempted here is how this one school's exemplification in practice of a theory born of the Block can legitimately be of import to schools which are Concurrent. The answer has already been implied. No matter how close together school and agency may be in time or space, they still remain separate, and the student still remains a human being, single in nature. If indeed through concurrence and fusion a single reality can be presented the student who is studying on the Block Plan where the gap appears to be very wide, then it may follow that the gap can be closed in a similar manner on the Concurrent Plan with its tighter structure.

As we explore the nature of concurrence of school and agency, we find that they do but meet at a point during the evolving of the teaching and learning process. At that point, a further step has to be taken, and in this essay this step is named "fusion." Both concurrence and fusion must remain just words to us in this introductory chapter, just implications of the direction we must take and the distance we must go for them to become understood. And, finally, the teaching and learning discussed in these pages take place in human processes through human relationships within a generative principle and can be, theoretically and practically, only another chapter in a human chronicle, the ending of which cannot be foreseen.

|

2

THE THEORY-PRACTICE DILEMMA

The problem of the duality of practice and theory became evident even before the actual separation of the professional school was made from the social agency. In anticipation of her descendants who might become highly educated in the separate schools, Frances Morse wrote that she feared the growth of generations of dry, academic social workers who thought they knew more than they really did.[1] Her opinion came in a letter responding to Mary Richmond's proposal in the 1897 Conference of Charities and Corrections, that a school of applied philanthropy be established apart from the social agencies.[2] This proposal meant that the teaching of young charity workers, a task up until this time carried on through apprenticeship, would be placed in the hands of educators, possibly even strangers. But for Mary Richmond, though the school would be separate from the agency, the two would go hand in hand; and the curriculum would be designed to meet the needs of agency, not of academy.

1. Frances Morse, A letter of rebuttal to paper given by Mary E. Richmond, in *Proceedings of National Conference of Charities and Corrections*, XXIV (1897), 187-88.
2. Mary E. Richmond, "The Need of a Training School in Applied Philanthropy," *Proceedings of the National Conference of Charities and Corrections*, XXIV (1897), 181-86.

The social workers of the new century, realizing the wisdom of the separating move, had no intentions of relinquishing entirely the responsibilities that were theirs for the future of social work. A summer school held in New York in 1898 under the auspices of the Charity Organization Society evolved five years later into the first full-time school of social work. Later still, this school was known as the New York School of Social Work, and it is now the Columbia University School of Social Work. By 1916, seven schools had opened their doors. All were known as "independent" schools, independent, that is, of the universities but not of the social agencies' concern and influence. All schools required for admission college graduation or its equivalent in education and experience.

After a few years, the universities became interested in the work of enterprising social workers and their field. They instituted courses and departments of social work in their graduate schools, stimulating a lively competition between the university-controlled and independent schools. Jesse Steiner, a professor at the University of North Carolina, who had welcomed the advent of social work into the university in 1920, and who had no doubt that the university could assume the education of social workers, wrote: "If the independent schools of social work have erred in concentrating too great attention upon the practical problems and immediate situations, the university courses in this field have usually gone to the opposite extreme. Will it be possible to build up courses that will avoid the shortcomings of both?"[3]

An English social worker, Elizabeth Macadam, came to the defense of the universities, too. Universities, she said, were a safeguard against the danger of political or any other kind of propaganda, for their whole tradition was against

3. Jesse F. Steiner, *Education for Social Work* (Chicago: The University of Chicago Press, 1921), pp. 46-47.

having students used for devious purposes.[4] Similar to Steiner's presentation of the possible overweighting of practice or theory was Macadam's comment that American social workers put too much emphasis upon techniques while English social workers put too little. What was needed, she said, was a race of teachers who were both philosophers and practitioners, and lucky indeed would be the school to secure such.

The independent schools, lacking in the weight and prestige of tradition and authority, were not lacking in creative, dedicated teachers. "Can this profession maintain a faith in its own material, its own labor, its own thinking, that will hold its own with established belief in the value of the academic degree?"[5] asked Virginia P. Robinson, a teacher of the independent school at Philadelphia. She saw a danger in the too early crystallization of social work education when principles would congeal before even beginning to be realized, in the too early classification and standardization of social work knowledge and methods. She hoped that the schools would experiment and continue to recognize their differences, one from the other. As social work education was close to fields beyond the ken of human knowledge, she considered it in a special position to proceed on its own.

The individual creativity of the independent schools and their teachers meeting with the important observations and questions of the universities and their professors provided a spirited beginning to the new profession. An imbalance of practice over theory or of theory over practice seemed to call forth attempts of both to control, to unite, to collaborate, with the social agency offering practice in the new relationship.

From the outset, social work educators, accustomed to

4. Elizabeth Macadam, *The Equipment of the Social Worker* (London: George Allen and Unwin, Ltd., 1925), p. 65.

5. Virginia P. Robinson, "Education for a Profession-in-the-Making," *Survey,* LII (September 1, 1924), 592.

the learning of apprenticeship, or of observation trips and excursions, assumed that "correlation" of class work and field work was a necessary condition for social work education. Through correlation, the experience of the field practice was brought to the classroom for discussion, and the theory of the classroom was taken to the field for application. Edith Abbott, of the independent school in Chicago, considered best the plan of four or five half days weekly in field practice along with school work. This plan wherein the exchange of theory and experience made within the same day or, as some other schools operated, within the same week, thus seeming almost to be simultaneous, came to be known as "Concurrent."

The majority of educators and social workers living in the large cities where agencies and schools could be reached by public transportation agreed with Edith Abbott. All of the seven independent schools adopted the Concurrent Plan. Other schools or departments, however, were not easily within reach of the agencies and had need of field work placements. The suggestion was made that, in such cases, students could be sent to field practice for one or two terms following a term in school. To this suggestion—later actualized in what is now known as the Block Plan—Edith Abbott said, "That this solution is unsatisfactory cannot be questioned. The correlation between field work and class work is impossible under such circumstances and the value of both is greatly lessened."[6] Most social workers, including the writer, agreed with Abbott up until recent years.

Some schools of that time, however, in their enterprising efforts to find an effective educational structure, experimented with a combination of Concurrent and Block. Smith College in 1918 went so far as to establish its school for

6. Edith Abbott, "Field-Work and the Training of the Social Worker," *Proceedings of the National Conference of Social Work,* XXXXII (1915), 621.

social service entirely on the Block Plan; it still is a Block Plan school and has never been other. In the first year of operation, classes without field work were held on the Smith College campus during the summer when the undergraduates were not there. Field work without classes was held during the regular academic year in agencies located in Boston, New York, Baltimore, and Philadelphia.

In the 1919-1920 catalog of the Smith College school is this description of its Block structure and its statement of belief:

The method of continuous practice is believed by the Sponsors to afford the best practical training. To become completely assimilated into the organization, the student must give full time to the work. To obtain the richest possible experience, the student should be on duty regularly and without interruption. In our opinion, practice work with social cases and social conditions cannot be carried on satisfactorily with intensive instruction, since it is not possible to regulate human problems, so that experience will run parallel with theoretical instruction. There is great value for drill and discipline as well as depth of experience in the uninterrupted practice and in the conformity of theoretical study which the present plan provides.[7]

From the beginning, this original Block Plan school refused the notion that human events in the field of practice could be so ordered as to correlate with classroom theory. In its plan, nevertheless, the Smith College school accepted its responsibility for the students during the eight months they were far from Northampton and erected a new structure. A relationship of the school to the students was maintained through assigned readings and gathering of thesis material. Occasional faculty visits to the field work agencies while the students were there also made a vital connection between school and students.

7. *Bulletin of the Smith College School for Social Service* (1919-1920).

A third plan, different from both the Concurrent and the Block, was suggested by Steiner but never was put into action. In his book, *Education for Social Work,* published in 1921, he outlined a plan patterned after medical education. The student of social work would have, along with his university work, a laboratory experience for testing his classroom knowledge. Later, he would have a clinic experience for observing the treatment of clients through a social work method carried out by a skilled practitioner. Finally, after he had completed his academic social work program, he would leave school and work full time in a social agency as an intern and for the first time begin to "treat" clients himself.

This plan of removing field work entirely from the department of social work and to place it with the agency in the concluding year would have solved the problem of the lack of field work placements at the University of North Carolina where Steiner taught and where the faculty's basic interest was in academic matters. The plan, however, was not instituted. Such action would have required a desertion of the department's belief in the necessity for the student to learn from both class and field within the framework of the university.

Social work educators who shared this belief that both class and field should come within the university framework were willing to admit that the field practice for the school's student had to be carried by agencies not under the direct control of the university or the independent school. In this way, they came face to face with another problem. The quality of the supervision offered the students was generally agreed to be in need of strengthening. To secure the kind of supervision necessary for students to begin to gain social work skill was not an easy assignment for educators to meet.

As might be expected and desired, the various schools and their faculties selected various ways of meeting the problem. Some advocated that the total control of the students' education be assured for the school by its establishing practice centers for field training and filling the supervisory jobs from the school's own personnel. Others thought the solution lay in the plan of sending school faculty into the existing social agencies to do the supervising. If the school could not supply enough supervisors, the agency field instructor (as the supervisor was called even in the 1920's) would be given a nominal position on the faculty and his conferences with the faculty would bring about a unity of agency and school. At any rate, no action should be taken, so these earnest pioneers insisted, that might accord to the agencies a position of superiority in their viewpoint and methods over those of the school.

On the other hand, there were social work teachers who claimed that the student should have the opportunity to experience the point of view and methods of the active social agency. The problems of control and of the quality of supervision were no less acute for them than for any of their colleagues in different schools. Their solution, however, was to keep the teacher in the school and the supervisor in the agency. The school would take the responsibility for offering to the supervisors the formal educational assistance they needed to meet the necessary qualifications to become supervisors of students. While permitting its students to risk the unknown of an agency not controlled by the school and of supervisors not on the school's staff, the school would remain in control of its own function of teaching and of its requirements for high standards in agency work with students and with clients before students could be placed.

In 1931, Maurice Karpf's book, *The Scientific Basis of Social Work*,[8] was published. Karpf wrote of field practice as emphasizing the trade aspects of social work and placing the schools at a disadvantage. As the agency really had the

8. Maurice J. Karpf, *The Scientific Basis of Social Work* (New York: Columbia University Press, 1931).

control, a conflict was set up in the minds of the students. He was convinced that there was no integration of the practical application of principles with their discussion in class and that the only true integration occurred in a school where the same person taught the student casework and also supervised his practice. He saw little to be lost through the separation of school and agency as on the Block Plan, and he saw little to be gained, either. Like Steiner before him, he advocated the postponement of field work until after the student had achieved an intellectual background and was better able to adjust to the problems of the field. Like Steiner before him, his plan was not put into practice.

Karpf's book makes it clear, too, that during these years of determining the educational structure of social work, there was no lack of course content. His detailed account of the nature of the knowledge needed for social workers to make adequate judgments touched upon many of the areas of content he considered important as the students' academic background for the profession. In the book's appendix, he reported that twenty-eight schools taught 147 different courses. This proliferation of content apparently arose from the efforts of the schools to meet the agencies' requests for the inclusion of particular knowledge and to meet the needs of what the treatment of clients seemed to require.

A revolutionary step toward a new concept of content in casework had been taken a year earlier with the publication of Virginia P. Robinson's book, *A Changing Psychology in Social Case Work*.[9] As long as the treatment of the individual client depended upon Mary Richmond's method of gathering information, making a diagnosis, and proposing a plan of treatment, the need for contentual knowledge seemed limitless. The questioning of the client to produce facts and the information needed by the social worker to interpret

9. Virginia P. Robinson, *A Changing Psychology in Social Case Work* (Chapel Hill: The University of North Carolina Press, 1930).

these facts or to diagnose led always to the need for more facts and more information. History-taking was a primary tool of the caseworker who tried to study the client as carefully and scientifically as possible. The impact of Robinson's book upon the social work world was electric. She said that not the content of the history or of the studies but the relationship of the client to the caseworker was at the core of helping.

It is difficult for the present generation of social workers to realize with what amazement this book's difference was received by social workers of that time. "Never again," wrote Bertha Reynolds, "would social workers be able peacefully to ignore personality relationships in case work as we have done."[10] With distress, she noted that by the time the worker had taken a voluminous history, the relationship had already been ruined! Her response, which recognized some of the startling implications of this book without embracing the change it required of her, was accompanied by complete resistance in other social workers to any proposal that offered no cause and effect explanation of human behavior and that apparently deserted the "scientific" method of helping.

When Reynolds reviewed the book a year later, still impressed with its contribution and its revolutionary nature but more questioning, she had evidently realized that the roots of Robinson's understanding of the client-worker relationship were deep in the psychology of Otto Rank. Reynolds had read a review Jessie Taft had written of an article by Rank.[11] Rank, as social workers were beginning to discover, was a lay psychotherapist who had been a member of Freud's inner circle and who had broken away from the

10. Bertha C. Reynolds, "A Changing Psychology in Social Case Work," *The Family*, XII (June, 1931), 113.

11. Jessie Taft, Review of "Die Analyse des Analytikers," by Otto Rank in *Psychoanalytic Review*, XVIII (October, 1931), 454. See also Jessie Taft, *Otto Rank* (New York: The Julian Press, Inc., 1958), pp. 164-65.

master to create his own philosophical psychology. Published in English as *Will Therapy and Truth and Reality*,[12] this part of his work attempted the difficult if not impossible job of putting into words the very process that underlies the content in the relationship of one human being to another.

The changing psychology in social casework, based on Rank's work, placed the client in the center of the stage and left the caseworker no longer all powerful. The right for the client to be himself and not what another would make of him was an exciting new thought and opened up for caseworkers an unknown future. This understanding of the relationship of worker and client as superseding the content of life histories threw the caseworker very much on his own, and the resultant loneliness was of concern not only to the critics of the new psychology but also to the creators at the Pennsylvania School of Social Work. A factor that would supply the more-than-self was missing.

In the first issue of the Pennsylvania school's *Journal of Social Work Process* in 1937, an article appeared which might now be accepted as the original statement of the functional generative principle.[13] This article supplied the missing factor—agency function. Of this article, Jessie Taft, who wrote it, said many years later: "The article on function has, perhaps, too much emotion in it, because actually the realization of function and its role in helping was a discovery for me, a genuine revelation. Also it fitted my bottom nature as relationship fitted Miss Robinson's. I think it was a little the way Rank felt when he realized 'will.' It illuminated everything."[14]

12. Otto Rank, *Will Therapy and Truth and Reality* (New York: Alfred A. Knopf, 1936).

13. Jessie Taft, "The Relation of Function to Process in Social Case Work," *Journal of Social Work Process*, I (November, 1937), 1-18. See also Virginia P. Robinson, ed., *Jessie Taft* (Philadelphia: University of Pennsylvania Press, 1962), pp. 206-26.

14. Jessie Taft in a personal letter to the author, dated January 3, 1955.

The caseworker was never again to be alone. Facing the client he could now have the agency's function to give life as well as limits to his activity and his client's. As the functional creators saw it, agency function as represented by the caseworker was the *given,* external to the client within the helping situation and against or toward which he could move with the given that was his internally. Requiring not only his will and his intellect, creative action that the caseworker hoped the client might achieve would require his impulses and emotions, too, and a willingness to submit to the positive nature of these givens, inner and outer. Efforts to gain complete mastery of life forces or any one of them leads to failure. In experiences partial to the client's life as in his relation to agency, he could begin to regain his strength and ability to meet his problems through meeting first with the worker the caring and the limitation of the agency's function and structure, and finding for himself what it was he wanted. The worker's control could not be of the client, only of himself as a professional helping person. This functional approach to casework was a process that could be taught and learned as the student himself lived a process not unlike that of the client.

One of the clearest presentations of another generative principle of social casework at that time was made by Fern Lowry, a teacher at the New York School of Social Work. She outlined a classification of the treatment phases to be taken after the worker had made a study and reached a diagnosis. There were three types of treatment: first, "those activities that are directed toward" enrichment or modification of the environment—a type that she named "manipulative"; second, "those activities that are directed toward" modifying the environment in order to affect individual relationships—treatment that she named "environmental"; and third, "those activities directed toward" modifying attitudes and relationships—treatment that she described as intensive, personal, psychological, or therapeutic.[15] Treatment, as is evident, was directed outward to change the client or his environment depending upon the worker's estimate of what he could do or needed to have done for him. As the caseworker could not wait to gather all the facts before making a hypothesis and beginning to treat the client, Lowry added that the stages of study, diagnosis, and treatment had to be interwoven.

Adherents of the diagnostic principle in their efforts to find and strengthen their casework method, which followed in outline that of a method of science, were critical of the Rankian psychology for its metaphysical aspects and of the functional generative principle for its close relation to a seemingly unscientific approach to human beings. Indirectly, they were asking that what the philosophers of the ages and psychologists of modern times were unable to do, functional caseworkers should have done. They should have been able to justify by reason or prove by experiment the truth of a statement like this one: "For to feel is to live but to reject feeling through fear is to reject the life process itself."[16]

Generations of students reading the article from which this sentence comes, or the sentence itself, have needed no justification by analysis, no proof by experiment. Each student of a functional school out of his own immediate experience feels its trueness for himself and learns. This epistemological and pedagogical unorthodoxy was puzzling to most social workers of the diagnostic schools, yet they did not deny the helpfulness of functional casework.

In 1942 two books were published which concerned themselves with social work education. One of them, *Train-*

15. Fern Lowry, "Current Concepts in Social Case-Work Practice," Part Two, *The Social Service Review,* XII (December, 1938), 593-94.
16. Jessie Taft, "Living and Feeling" (taken from *Child Study,* January, 1933), mimeographed.

ing for Skill in Social Case Work,[17] edited by Virginia
Robinson, was published in time for Bertha C. Reynolds,
author of *Learning and Teaching in the Practice of Social
Work,*[18] to make use of it in her writing. In Robinson's
book, the fundamental likeness of the individual's process in
learning, being helped, or being supervised, to that of the
natural growth process and the fundamental differences
among the functions of teaching, casework, and supervision
were presented as a further evolving of the functional generative principle. The psychological background throughout is
that of Rank. Reynolds, on the other hand, who had by this
time firmly established herself as a teacher of diagnostic casework based on Freudian psychoanalysis, constructed her psychological understanding of the teaching-learning process not
out of Freud's work but Morgan's *Child Psychology.*[19] One
might ask whether a single psychology might not serve as
base for both practice and education for practice.

The knowledge and the skill of social workers, either
diagnostic or functional, were by the late 1930's not always
welcomed by the universities when practitioners joined
departments of social work faculties. Although the university
professor who had dedicated his life to teaching in these
departments was often a skilled and devoted teacher, he
usually was not skilled in casework practice that by this
time was being sought by the students and by agencies even
in rural areas. The impact of the practitioner-teacher upon
the graduate schools is evident in an article[20] written in
1939 by Roy M. Brown, then Director, Division of Public
Welfare and Social Work at the University of North

17. Virginia P. Robinson, ed., *Training for Skill in Social Case Work*
(Philadelphia: University of Pennsylvania Press, 1942).

18. Bertha Capen Reynolds, *Learning and Teaching in the Practice
of Social Work* (New York: Farrar and Rinehart, 1942).

19. John Jacob Brooke Morgan, *Child Psychology* (3rd ed.; New
York: Farrar and Rinehart, Inc., 1942).

20. "Education for Public Welfare and Social Work," *Social Forces,*
XVIII (October, 1939), 65-70.

Carolina. With the technician taking over in the departments of social work and the formation of university schools of social work separate from the graduate schools, he foresaw the lowering of standards and a concentration upon the teaching of techniques.

In England, Elizabeth Macadam agreed with Brown when she wrote again of this university-profession problem. By 1945 she conceded that the fears of practitioners concerning the university's inability to supply practical experience had not been unfounded. But the university, she said, was reluctant to award a degree and to dilute standards for the sake of a profession that did not know even its own requirements. The university knew well of its value to the student: "It is hardly possible to overestimate the value of the university spirit during his introduction to the hard facts of economic conditions. When in his historical studies he projects himself into the life of the past and relates it to the present he gains strength and maturity to judgment which will be of value to him in the future in which he hopes to play a part."[21] The social work faculty had to grow up to a trust in its own academic capabilities and its own knowledge and skill before it could risk trusting the university; the academic faculty had to grow to a trust in itself and the university to permit the appearance among them of the new and unformed professional school with its practitioner-teachers.

The practitioner-teachers were hard at work on some of the tremendous problems facing them. Assuming from the start that social work education had as its goal the transmitting of both knowledge and skill to its students, the relation of class and field continued to be in the forefront of their practice and deliberations. Recognizing her fragmentary approach to this difficult subject, Goldie Basch (later Dr. Goldie Basch Faith) developed a paper in response to

21. Elizabeth Macadam, *Social Servants in the Making* (London: George Allen and Unwin, Ltd., 1945), p. 37.

her own question: "Which elements combine to create this integration of theory and practice?"[22] She located the answer in the relation of school and agency as she discussed her experience in teaching in a school operating on the Concurrent Plan. She considered the processes involved in admissions, school-agency relations, adviser-supervisor conferences, and the student's use of his own cases in class. Working out of the functional principle, she turned to both theory and practice in the processes of relationship necessarily formed to teach and to learn knowledge and skill in the casework function.

Although Basch was working out of and upon the Concurrent Plan, she like other social work educators did not attempt to tackle the meaning of "concurrence." Although they seemed to assume that correlation of class and field, integration of school and agency, and continuity of learning were necessary conditions for effective education, concurrence was never questioned. The Concurrent Plan somehow held within it the unquestioned assumption that concurrence meant school and agency existing at the same time, which was generally felt to be "good." The Block Plan schools (for Smith College was by this time in the early 1940's joined by two others) in the face of this assumption and their structure seemed to be forever estopped from offering their students whatever this "good" element was in concurrence.

Despite their inability to meet concurrent conditions in terms of the Concurrent Plan, more schools considered the Block Plan in order to meet the increased enrollments following World War II. In the attempt to meet this increased demand, which necessitated an increased number of field work placements, a committee was organized by the

22. Goldie Basch, "Class Room and Field Work: Their Joint Contribution to Skill," *Training for Skill in Social Case Work,* ed. Virginia P. Robinson (Philadelphia: University of Pennsylvania Press, 1942), p. 32.

American Association of Schools of Social Work (later the Council on Social Work Education) in 1948 to discuss the Block Plan. Participants from both Concurrent and Block Plan schools gathered to explore the subject. At the conclusion of the meeting held in 1948, the committee recommended continuation of the exploration of practical problems which it had begun and on which it had made progress. In the 1949 meeting, the focus changed to a clarification of terms and a forming of definitions. The discussions moved from the particular of the Block Plan to the general of social work education on any plan, and then to how the Block Plan school could meet these goals. The committee finished its work affirming the educational potential of the Block Plan, a step that had not been taken so positively heretofore.

The committee's positive step and the acute need of the schools for field work placements did not make it easy for schools to shift from Concurrent to Block or to open on the Block, not just because of administrative difficulties but also because of the resistance encountered. At the University of North Carolina, for example, faculty and supervisors saw little in favor of such a change. Faculty members who traveled to agencies in other states for conferences with supervisors while still on the Concurrent Plan, and who knew that despite the predicted growth of the Chapel Hill community, expansion of the school was limited by the number of placements within commuting distance, still did not want to change to the Block. Students who rode train, bus, and car back and forth each week to agencies 150 miles away and who at the time complained of the trips often requested still farther away placements for their second year. Executives and supervisors of field work agencies were apprehensive about what this new and radical plan would mean to them when they had to assume full-time responsibility for the student. Under the leadership and conviction of Dean

Arthur E. Fink, the school did make the shift and, in the year 1950-1951, became a Block Plan school.

There seems to be no way as yet to judge the educational values of one plan in respect to the other, or one set of reasons for the use of this plan or that one. Any school has to have field placements for its existence. If one acceptable educational plan will make possible the needed placements and the other acceptable educational plan will not, the school's choice of plan is obvious. The burden upon a school is not the "ought" urging the choice for a respectable reason, but, after choosing, it is the obligation to provide effective and sound education within the chosen structure.

The requirements for all schools of social work were set up by the Council on Social Work Education in its manual for accrediting standards issued in 1952 and revised in 1953. In the 1953 manual[23] and in the official statement of curriculum policy adopted on October 19, 1962, the requirements plainly and simply pertain to all schools whether on Block Plan or Concurrent Plan in respect to their relation to the field agency. A school is expected to have a partnership with the field work agency where a student is placed and yet is expected to retain control of the educational function; a school is expected to reach an agreement with the field work agency in goals, theories, and methods; and a school is expected to be willing to help the field work agency supervisor provide the quality of supervision a student has the right to expect. The way in which these elements are provided may and should differ from school to school as long as the common concern of all schools is a relating of school and field for the student's integration of learning and continuity of experience.

"Correlation" of class and field is not included in these

23. Council on Social Work Education, Manual for Accrediting Standards for Graduate Schools of Social Work (June, 1953), mimeographed.

requirements. It may well be, as the early Block Plan faculty of Smith College pointed out, that correlation is impossible on any plan if by correlation is meant the ordering of human events to meet the theory. Correlation is impossible on the Block Plan if by correlation is meant the weekly interchange of field experiences and classroom theory. The structure of correlation may have to remain with the Concurrent Plan faculties to explore by way of either definition and to make available to their students, if they can. What is ruled out for the student of the Block Plan school is his learning in the school's *classroom* during the field work terms, although learning from the school during these terms can become available to him, as we shall see later.

Whatever their field work plan, whatever their generative principle, social work educators continued in the 1950's wrestling with the duality and how to meet it in their programs.

In the 1950's, structural devices erected to bring about integration were revived and practiced. Some schools sent faculty members into the agencies to supervise the school's students. Other schools hired the personnel for student supervision in the agencies. Rumors of schools' opening their own practice agencies were heard, though no records of such openings have been found. These structural devices kept the control in the school by reaching into the agencies with its actual physical presence. One can but recall Virginia Robinson's remark of many years past that the presence of a supervisor in the agency, yet outside its discipline, must create acute problems for both.[24]

Integration by structure was also described by Hilda C. M. Arndt,[25] once again to insure the school's control and

24. Virginia P. Robinson, "Organization of Field Work in a Professional School," *The Family*, I (October, 1920), 3.

25. Hilda C. M. Arndt, "The Learner in Field Work," Paper read at Council on Social Work Education, 4th Program Meeting, Buffalo, N. Y. (January 26, 1956), mimeographed.

this time with the added invitation to mutuality through inclusion. Agency supervisors were integrated into the entire teaching faculty by having faculty status conferred upon them, by presenting material to the classes, taking courses in supervision, developing relationships with various faculty members, having access to all course outlines, objectives, bibliographies, teaching records, and assignments. Tutorial supervision of the new supervisor of students was offered by the faculty to help him attain an identification with the school as a member of the faculty. This route to "integration," one must observe, might result in a desired "togetherness" and at the same time entail a loss of identity for both teacher and supervisor. Such a loss of individual identity may be part of what this plan desires to achieve; to the outsider, it appears difficult to discern what identity would take its place for the student.

For Louis Lehrman, the way for school and agency to integrate was for class and field to integrate by making the conceptual thinking as alike as possible.[26] It must surely be so that no educational plan could be helpful for the student were the school and the agency to work from opposing ideologies, each of which is determinedly taught the student, one at the school and the other at the agency. An administrative agreement concerning standards and general educational viewpoint would undergird the respective responsibilities of school and of agency for the training process to follow. A professional agreement concerning principles of casework and supervision would also seem necessary. Agreement in either case could go only "as far as possible"; complete agreement is hardly likely. Conceptual agreement, however close, could not induce an integration of school and agency if this integration entails, as it does for most educators, a union in relationship.

26. Louis J. Lehrman, "The Integration of Class and Field in Professional Education," *Social Casework*, XXXIII (June, 1952), 254.

The formation of such a relationship proved to be a thornier problem than Mary Richmond had envisaged in school and agency going hand in hand. There was general agreement with Arlien Johnson, who expressed it as an interrelatedness of school and agency necessary for a student to achieve integrity.[27] There was general agreement that, as going hand in hand had through the years revealed pressures on first one hand and then the other, the control had to be taken by the school, not the agency. There was general disagreement on how the school could assume this control and yet maintain a sense of mutuality. The problem remained as to how such interrelatedness could be brought about.

In the writings of Lois Sentman[28] and Annette Garrett,[29] both from Block Plan schools, came the characterization of the faculty adviser to the student in field work as a "catalyst." Sentman saw the faculty representative as helping the student relate to the supervisor and the supervisor to the student. What is of special import for us is that these teachers were reporting from their own experiences of an acute shift that occurred when the faculty adviser visited student and supervisor in agency. Neither of them followed through with an exploration of the nature of this shift and rested on the explanation of "catalyst." Perhaps a chemical can act as a catalyst; one must wonder whether a human being can do so. It is more likely, and we shall try to go further into this very point later, that a human being is affected by the process himself and he cannot directly change another person who chooses change for himself.

In the Concurrent Plan school where the student's turn-

27. Arlien Johnson, "Educating Professional Social Workers for Ethical Practice," *Social Service Review*, XXIX (June, 1955), 129.
28. Lois Sentman, "The Role of the Faculty Representative in Field Work," *Social Service Review*, XXIII (September, 1949), 337-46.
29. Annette Garrett, "Learning Through Supervision" in Vol. XXIV (February, 1954) of *Smith College Studies in Social Work*.

ing point with the adviser may be as acute as any on the Block Plan, yet without the supervisor's presence in agency on the same day, the sense of the shift in relation to both may appear less vivid than on the Block Plan. Louis Lehrman, of a Concurrent Plan school, wrote that the school-agency relationship is a co-operative one—with the school in control and the agency co-operative and adjunctive.[30] From another Concurrent Plan school, Laura Downes proposed that the casework teacher (also the student's field work adviser) and the agency supervisor collaborate.[31] Collaboration cannot be completely mutual, however, for as Downes sees it, the school yields less of its own wholeness than does the agency. One might wonder how the "more or less" of yielding can be ascertained when an individual is the one who must do it. The important point of what Downes says to us is that both school and agency do yield of their own wholeness in the interest of their relationship on behalf of the student who is learning from both.

As we come now to recent times, we still have a sense of the existing problem and of the efforts made and being made to solve it, and we pause to reflect. It may be that Karpf was right in his conviction that the only integration of school and agency he ever saw was in a school where the same person taught the student casework in the classroom and supervised his practice in the agency. Or perhaps some of the early social workers were right in their conviction about the never-to-be-improved-upon method of apprenticeship. The core of the difficulty revealed again and again in this brief review of literature on the subject is how to unite the two halves of professional education ever since it was split.

30. Lehrman, "Integration of Class and Field," *Social Casework*, p. 254.

31. Laura B. Downes, "Collaboration Between the School and the Agency in Professional Education for Social Work," *Journal of Social Work Process*, X (1959), 21-26.

One alternative to integration of school and agency as a way of healing the split is in a recent suggestion by Werner Boehm,[32] as it was suggested in 1921 by Steiner and in 1931 by Karpf. The internship plan, renamed currently the "practicum," meets the problem of the split by eliminating it. With the academic work completed during a continuum of two undergraduate and two graduate years of study to be followed by a final year of full-time employment in an agency away from the school's control, the need for correlation, integration, or collaboration simply does not exist. The separation is structurally complete.

Another alternative, the one that shall be proposed here, meets the problem of the split by affirming it with a clear-cut functional difference maintained between the institution of learning and the institution of helping. They can through their representatives come to concur by their contemporaneousness and their agreeing conceptually as far as possible—but they do not become integrated. It is at a point of concurrence that two functionally separate representatives, one of school and one of agency, can take a step that enables the student to find before him a fusion of school-agency, a single reality.

This second alternative requires the student to be offered his classroom work and his field work serially in the course of his two years of graduate study. He is one person and will, if he is to be a caseworker, engage himself both intellectually and experientially in field and class. If he does not need both class and field in alternating fashion, then a radical and revolutionary change in educational theory and structure would be in order. If he does, and most social workers are convinced that he does, then our heritage and our history have led us to this place and we have much work to do.

32. Werner Boehm, *Objectives of the Social Work Curriculum of the Future* (The Comprehensive Report of the "Curriculum Study": Council on Social Work Education, Vol. I [New York, 1959]).

3

THE NEED
FOR A SINGLE REALITY

Now, as in the past that is our heritage, we come to the problem of how it can be that a student who is asked to learn in two places can complete his educational experience with his academic and experiential learning integrated within him. Indeed, within these two places of learning, school and agency, are many segments and, in view of them, the wonder is that learning ever eventuates. The wonder may even increase when we consider that the direction this essay will take in tackling the problem is marked by the conception of man's nature as single. From within this single nature, so we say, man presses to discover truth for himself in relation to his external reality. In order for him to choose at all, in living and in learning, this external reality is itself single or, in his eyes, it becomes single when he reaches the actual point of choosing.

What we need to do now is to begin at the beginning to clarify what we mean by this conception of man's single nature and his relation to external reality. The beginning seems far away from the social work student and social work, for it is at the core of life that we look first. Each individual began life as a single cell containing an ageless heritage and pulsating with life of its very own. This original life impulse, so soon a cell dividing and growing, moves toward more life and, with its cells integrated into a being called "man," seeks fulfillment of its potential.

The individual-in-the-making as a multi-celled zygote is separate and alone. It needs nourishment and finds it in the womb of the mother, need and satisfaction of need being one. When simple infusion of nutriment is not adequate, it attaches itself to the uterine wall. It grows still larger; it builds itself a placenta. Always it is itself, separate and alone, for always between it and the mother is the foetal tissue. Never again will it be closer to another human being and never again farther away.

At the time of birth, the great separation is more than that of the baby from the mother; it is also that of two individuals ending one relationship and beginning a new one, face to face. After the experience of this separation, after the experience of the first shock of a totally different locale of living, after his reunion in enveloping arms, he begins to discover that never again will his needs be met without waiting. Never again will the outside of himself exist entirely for him.

Out in the open where he can be seen, the young human being displays what seems very much like a dual nature. He can take or he can refuse. He can smile or he can cry. He can be angry or he can be loving. With consciousness and his developing will, he can move toward his mother positively and unitingly or he can move away negatively and separately. He has the power within him, a power called the will, to inhibit or to fulfill the potential of life that is his. This is a two-sided individual, surely.

But it may be, and this is how we find it, that the impulse is single, springing from the core of life; and the will that rises to carry out the impulse is single, also, though it can move negatively or positively. His awakening intellect does not separate from his deepening emotions; they interact continually. All this is what is given man and he alone can decide what he will do with integrating it, what direction he will take, and what his own characteristic pattern will be.

As this human being grows, the realities within and outside him seem to become even more complex. He begins to discover persons important to him who are away from his home, and he begins to feel strange emotions, the fears and the joys of seeking friends or being sought. The amazing new impulse of sex arises within him, and he is fearful of where it will lead him if he lets it. He grows to discover it is his to use and in a large measure to control. The exciting world of intellectual attainment begins to open to him. And at the same time, the childhood parental "no" and the wagon that could not be fixed become the car that cannot be bought and the mountain that cannot be climbed. Along with all the accomplishments of mind, and body, and emotion, come the unattainable, the unmoving, the block to the onrushing will. The impact he feels heightens the sense of self, the single individual thwarted and having to come to terms with the inevitable, inside and outside himself.

The great paradox is that, alone by nature and alone with his inner turmoil and his inner strengths, the individual cannot grow or learn or reach fulfillment by himself. He needs another human being who can be for him the single external reality he seeks.

In the therapy of life, parent, friend, or partner becomes the other person he needs, each in a different time and place. He lives in a group, he goes to school in a group, he works in a group, he exchanges experiences with a group. But when he seeks the healing of life through the relationships it offers, he seeks one person. Out of the multiplicity of his inner and outer life, the route to the integration he hopes to find seems to him to lie in his relationship with another person who can care for him, who can release him from the pain of such great individuality, who can affirm for him his very being through union. The other person also has needs and also has limitations. To find the union with the other and to find the integration within himself he so greatly wants, to reach the fulfillment of the potential he has in him, he must yield in the face of the unchangeable nature of this other. He must yield his own strong will and permit his feeling to be expressed, for only with feeling can he unite in relationship.

In yielding, the word that means not submission or defeat, he is himself, whole and single. He is a man of will and feeling and impulse and intellect who, united within, yields his grip on intactness and chooses the path to life and growth which for the moment lies in his uniting with another. This moment, temporary as it must be in friendship or sexual union or in creative work, provides the therapy of life. In it is the healing of the split, the bringing together of the torn pieces. For most of living, this therapy of life itself is enough as another step in the fulfillment of the inner potential is taken. And still within him is the urge for more and fuller life in ending or changing this relationship and in meeting alone new impacts, new unions, new integration. Still within him is his "inner pressure after truth."[1]

There may come a time when the therapy of life is not enough, when the confusions and problems are such that the individual moves in need toward professional help. His original impulse for life, his will to carry it out, his intellect to comprehend his situation, his emotions so expressive of his very self are all still his, torn and upset as he may be. Could the professional helper offer him the therapy of life as he has once known it, offer him a relationship with the caring and the limitations he cannot now achieve in his social life, he might once again come through to a new vigor

1. Otto Rank, *Will Therapy and Truth and Reality* (New York: Alfred A. Knopf, 1945), p. 220.

and a new wholeness. But a professional helper cannot offer personal relationships to the clients of his agency.

Nor can the teacher in a school of social work offer personal relationships to the students who, although they come not for help as a client to a social agency, nevertheless have an expressed desire to learn. This they cannot do alone. They, too, must move into school and find there the impact of a new world and of new relationships. They will find there that they are asked to learn theory in one place, practice in another, as if they were so split between intellect and feeling. They will find the uncrossable mountains that will not be changed for them. It may be that the therapy of life in relationship is not unrelated to the student who seeks to learn rather than to be healed. The fact remains, however, that should he live out the same process of growth through relationship that he has lived out over and over again with the important people of his growing years, he may expect and will not find that kind of personal relationship with the school faculty.

What then can be done by the professional helper, whether he is a caseworker or teacher? He can offer within the confines of the social agency or the university's school of social work the opportunity for client or student to live out his life's process with another person in a relationship that is functional and artificial. This approach raises many questions among those in the field of social work who have elected to work out of another generative principle, and that other way of working has raised questions among those who are functional. The heat of the battle is long since over, but questions need still to be raised and observations made.

As has been said here, the singleness of the human being arises, in our premise, from the original source of life which is his alone; he moves, as he grows and learns, toward the integration, and making whole of a self that will fulfill his original potential. The integrated self can inhibit future growth or can bring growth into being, can permit the momentary break-up of its integration in order to admit another or to admit new learning or can remain intact and alone. New integrations, then, will take place if the individual so acts to change himself in a way that is "spontaneous and irreversible movement toward fulfillment," the "integration of the organism's potential for development."[2]

A quite different premise for the nature of the original life impulse and its integration is presented by Charlotte Towle, a social work educator, in her book, *The Learner in Education for the Professions*. She says, "The organism's basic motive is the impulse to survive. Learning is the organism's means to survival, and hence an enduring propensity. To understand learning, therefore, it must be regarded as an organic process through which the organism strives to remain intact, to preserve itself as a whole."[3] From this premise, Towle develops her theory of education for social work with its underlying psychological implications. Integration of learning is part of the striving of the individual to keep himself intact and requires of him the ability to relate things to each other and to put the parts together into a whole. When the learner can see this whole as greater than the sum of its parts, he has not only achieved integration, he is on his way to becoming creative.

When educators like Towle speak of integration of content, they apparently mean that the student makes into one intelligible whole all the various courses and readings and lectures to which he has been exposed. His creative ability is in the arranging and rearranging of this very content into different configurations. The student possesses a certain integrative capacity that differs in degree from other stu-

2. Jessie Taft, "A Conception of the Growth Process Underlying Social Casework Practice," in *Jessie Taft,* ed. Virginia P. Robinson (Philadelphia: University of Pennsylvania Press, 1962), p. 328.
3. Charlotte Towle, *The Learner in Education for the Professions* (Chicago: The University of Chicago Press, 1954), p. 27.

dents and, when exceeded, leads to fear and anxiety. Consistent with this understanding of the original life impulse and of integration in learning, educators must be careful not to exceed the student's integrative capacity. Life that is for survival will be life on guard against outer stresses, strains, or attacks. The educator evaluates the student's capacity and provides the bulwarks.

From the point of view taken in this essay, however, life that is for the fulfillment of an inner potential rather than for survival only, is life that has its own direction and seeks its own truth. Integration is the making whole of the self not simply through the mind or the will or the external manipulation of content but through the working together of the will, the intellect, the feelings, the impulse—all in the one human individual who moves toward fulfillment. The creative use of the self in achieving such integration can be anyone's, in his own way and to his own ability. He possesses the power to act, not just react; to move ahead or to inhibit. He is the one who performs the miracle of transforming content into experience and experience into content, through his own act of learning.

Such learning requires a process of relationship with a teacher. The student who has his own strength to act as well as to react to the outside nevertheless cannot learn or become whole all by himself. He needs another and this other the educator becomes. As the student pushes toward finding what is truth for himself, he needs the outside that he can meet and that, if it corresponds to his inner self, is truth for him. Only he can make this correspondence; only he can make the outside into an integral part of himself. His teacher, then, offers him not "truth" but reality.

Social workers are often of the opinion that they must know what is true for their clients or students, and this attempt to achieve a definitive knowledge is confined to no one school of thought. We seem to need to be able to state with certainty what is so for the other and why. Yet doubt is always with us. Can we really know? It may be that truth is, as we are saying here, discovered by correspondence of statement with fact. Unlike many philosophers who agree that truth is ascertained through such correspondence, we add that psychological truth is reached by the individual act of correspondence, the act of formulating through feeling an inner "statement" or recognition, of the self's meeting in truth the outer fact or reality. This approach to the discovery of truth when extended to a theory of helping people, such as in casework, acknowledges that the client himself has the power given to him to find and to choose his own truth. To make this acknowledgment and to act upon it as a helping person is difficult to comprehend and to risk. "Objective" truth or knowledge somehow seems safer.

To gain objective knowledge of the client, Werner Boehm in his volume, *The Social Casework Method in Social Work Education,* employs Towle's presentation of Freud's ego psychology and offers a scheme of assessing the client in relation to the problem. The caseworker is to take certain steps, which are, briefly: determine the nature of the problem, determine whether or not the casework method is appropriate, determine which role performance of the client is impaired and what use of resources, inner and outer, he has made, and determine which factors are amenable to change.[4] In planning the activities designed to carry out the treatment of the client, Boehm says, "In the light of the assessment a plan of action is formulated which spells out explicitly the steps to be taken in professional intervention and the results which are to be expected. The plan identifies approaches which seem to be the most appropriate and indi-

4. Werner Boehm, *The Social Casework Method in Social Work Education* (A Project Report of the "Curriculum Study": Council on Social Work Education, Vol. X [New York, 1959]), pp. 132-34.

cates the timing and the sequence of professional activities designed to produce more effective role performance."[5]

Boehm's theory, as it applies to helping through casework, obtains also for the education of caseworkers. The student's capacity for integration is assessed and the program developed to provide what would be appropriate experiences for him and for all students, keeping stress at a minimum and timed as to degree of simplicity or complexity of the content of learning and the order and rate of its repetition. Identifiable facts about the student's capacity to withstand the interacting forces impinging upon him in learning would need to be increasingly determined in order to plan the educative program necessary for appropriate action by the educators.

The simple question which might well be raised is this: where is the client's—or the student's—own determination?

Boehm as a social worker might not reply to this question as would the behaviorist psychologists who extend further than he the principle of determinism. It is likely they would say that the client or student has no determination of his own, for man is caught in a web of past events over which he has no control. That he is or can become free to choose and to act in determining his own direction is an illusion. B. F. Skinner in *Science and Human Behavior* writes: "The hypothesis that man is not free is essential to the application of scientific method to the study of human behavior. The free inner man who is held responsible for the behavior of the external biological organism is only a prescientific substitute for the kinds of causes which are discovered in the course of a scientific analysis. All these alternative causes lie *outside* the individual. . . . The environment determines the individual even when he alters the environment."[6]

5. *Ibid.,* p. 135.
6. B. F. Skinner, *Science and Human Behavior* (New York: The Macmillan Company, 1953), pp. 447-48.

It is entirely consistent with this hypothesis that Skinner and James G. Holland have devised a teaching method in which the environment determines the individual. Their book, *The Analysis of Behavior,* is itself the teaching structure, a program for self-instruction whereby with the book and a teaching machine, the student learns the science of behavior and its application in the prediction and control of human beings. The authors foresee their science being expanded to such diverse fields as "social behavior and psychopharmacology, space flight and child care, education and psychotherapy."[7] Undoubtedly, social work could be included.

With the behaviorists' interest in stimulus and response, conditioning and reinforcement, the student's behavior in the learning of content has been carefully analyzed and the stresses of learning almost entirely eliminated by the use of book and teaching machine. The book's content is arranged to move slowly from the simple to the more complex concepts, with repetitions worded and spaced to meet the student's predicted behavior in learning. He is told at the outset that in responding to the statements by filling in the blanks, he can nearly always be right and move always at his own pace. Continued success is a fundamental principle of this theory of learning.

Skinner and Holland's attempt to make learning into a science would seem to have brought about an operation as close to a mechanical one as could be imagined for human beings. The power in the hands of the programmer appears limitless, and he avoids any complications of human relationships in learning and teaching. While the student's behavior is being thus predicted and controlled, the student himself is learning to predict and control the behavior of other human beings.

For the social worker who remembers a cardinal tenet, or

7. James G. Holland and B. F. Skinner, *The Analysis of Behavior* (New York: McGraw-Hill Book Co., 1961), p. vii.

perhaps cliché, of social work—that the individual be free to choose and to go in his own direction—this method and content of learning, as it is now being advanced vigorously by the behaviorists on many fronts, would be unacceptable. The behaviorists' student seems little freer than Pavlov's dog—and indeed Skinner and Holland list Pavlov as one of their sources. The behaviorists' student marks down his answers as predicted in reference to the controls exerted. Actually he could stop anywhere along the way and throw away the book and machine if he decided he did not want to learn how to control and predict human behavior. In all likelihood, should the authors of the book and inventors of the machine hear of this student's protest, they would revise the program to make certain that no student would ever again exhibit such deviant and negative reactions.

Skinner's student is unfree. He is unfree within himself and has no opportunity to realize it. His doubts and his fears, his confusion and his turmoil, he must deny in an experience in which he is always right. He must also deny his strengths and his abilities to react upon outside forces as well as reacting to them. He must deny his life impulse and creativity, for the stresses have been eliminated and he has had no part in eliminating them, or even in meeting them. To be unfree within oneself is the greatest captivity of all. Does man *have* to be unfree?

Out of the functional generative principle with its entirely different perspective from that of the deterministic psychologies, Anita J. Faatz developed her understanding of the nature of choice.[8] She agrees that often the proud assumption is made that the individual has as a natural state of his being the freedom to choose and that the impositions of life and of helper or teacher restrict that freedom. Rather than being free, Faatz finds that the human being who is the

8. Anita J. Faatz, *The Nature of Choice in Casework Process* (Chapel Hill: The University of North Carolina Press, 1953).

client is actually unfree, caught in the problems and pressures that he has brought to the agency in seeking help.

But diametrically opposed to Skinner, Faatz maintains that man can become free. In order to become free, free to choose and to act, he may engage in a process with a helper to learn what it is to be free. Freedom of choice, in this view, is not the gift of nature or of a benevolent society or person; nor is it forever withheld from man by his nature, his past, or his environment. It must be earned, for it can be earned, by each individual.

Such inner freedom is earned in relation to an outer reality that the individual cannot change or control and yet which holds for him, if he will take of it, the life and growth he seeks in fulfilling his potential. The outer reality in the helping or teaching processes is held by the human helper or teacher, and the path to inner freedom is through relationship. To the deterministic psychologist, this method with its dependence upon process and relationship is both old-fashioned and slow. In fact he would add that the student suffers unnecessarily from making mistakes, being held to expectations, and meeting deadlines not of his own making.

That the student has more than a mind for clever memorizing, more to learn than specific content printed sentence by sentence as truth, and more to integrate in learning than the fitting together of pieces of a puzzle apparently is irrelevant to learning when the purpose is to gain scientific accuracy and speed in the prediction and control of human behavior. But the behaviorist's reliance upon the human will and intellect and the exclusion of feelings and impulses and emotions, is, once again, entirely consistent. The possibility of the earning of an inner freedom by the student does not appear important when prediction and control of human behavior are his goals.

For the student who wants to become an integrated, creative caseworker, our method of teaching him to help troubled human beings who have feelings and impulses, emotions, and will and intellect should be at least as consistent in its way as the behaviorist's method is in its.

Process in relationship *is* old-fashioned; it is as old as man himself, as are mistakes and expectations and deadlines. By non-functional social workers, we might be asked: but how do you know the individual client or student is strong enough to engage in such a process? We can only answer that we do not know; we cannot predict, even though he has lived this process many times in life, however old or young he may be. The critics will point out that he will erect defenses against the stresses of outside pressures and fears of outside dangers; they will say that since these defenses inhibit learning, what of them? We would say in reply that it takes strength to defend oneself and that this very strength may act upon the outside that seems so fearful as well as being acted upon by it. In our book, "resistance" is a more exact term than "defense," for it carries with it a sense of the active expression of individual strength, albeit negatively directed, rather than a defensive cover of weakness. In the process of learning or of being helped, the strength spent in resisting what he as a client or student has come seeking, and sometimes paying money for, may be shifted by the individual himself to an expenditure of that same vigor in positive action and relationship.

Rudolf Ekstein, a psychologist, and Robert S. Wallenstein, a psychiatrist, both Freudian-oriented members of the staff of the Menninger School of Psychiatry, made such a discovery for themselves in their book, *The Teaching and Learning of Psychotherapy,*[9] giving credit to social work for having seen it first. When they supervised psychotherapists-in-training and used psychoanalytic terminology, they found that they tended to regard the student as a patient. When

9. Rudolf Ekstein and Robert S. Wallenstein, *The Teaching and Learning of Psychotherapy* (New York: Basic Books, 1958).

they shifted to the language of supervision which is familiar to some social workers in such words as "resistance," "beginning," "ending," "identification with function," they relinquished their diagnosing the student's behavior as an illness that called for treatment by themselves or some other therapist and saw him rather as an individual resisting the learning process. They came to the conclusion that they could have utilized more than they had such an understanding of resistance and could have emphasized illness less.

For these two doctors, more than their language had shifted. We would say that the student was accorded his rightful place as chief actor in the learning process and add that perhaps the patient belonged in this place, too. The shift to a regard for the student as chief actor (Rank's term) and the psychiatrist-supervisor as standing in the wings is difficult to make; it would be far harder for these doctors to make this same shift for the patient. Yet perhaps some day they will make another discovery that will have to do with the single nature of man in the common human process of relationship wherein even the neurotic patient is the one who knows.

Like many practitioners, the beginning student of social casework finds it difficult, too, to *be* rather than to *know*. He has come to school with a zeal to change the client, in the name of helping him, from what he is into what the student would have him be. The student caseworker places himself in the spotlight, for he is the one who must know the client and decide upon the steps to be taken in making him happy once again. Without this desire or this strong will to change the other, the student would have elected some other occupation where he could create by changing objects into a likeness of himself or his projections. The purpose of the profession that he has chosen is, instead, to help people. To be creative with people, he begins by trying to change them despite the fact that he comes to school saying the words, "I want to help people help themselves."

What transpires for all of us who come into social work and who have been students of the functional generative principle is that a shift does have to take place. This inner shift is not simply of attitudes, of enlarging compassion, of attaining dispassion, it is a fundamental change within the self from being the creator of the other person to being the creator of oneself. Strangely enough, although each student must make such a shift, it seems time and again that to be his own creator, to grow to his own fulfillment is what he has wanted in the first place. He has come asking to become a caseworker, to become a helping person, to become someone a troubled person might turn to in need. Yet it is with shock that he receives the word, in one way or another, that asks him to begin to grow up to be just that—a helping person. He cannot become both a helping person and a controller of people, a caseworker and a puppet-master.

The student has far to go to become the caseworker who sees the client as the one who decides upon his own direction, who knows himself better than anyone else can know him, who is acting in relationship and not simply reacting. He is to become the helper who no longer seeks the client's weaknesses in the moments of stress, who no longer devises explicit steps of intervention into the client's life with professional activities or determines what results can be expected. He will become the helper who contains his own will to change the client even by the seemingly mild means of contentual interpretations. He will become a helper whose self will be used by the client. In a functional capacity and not a personal one, he will be the client's "other," no less real in relationship than would be any other human being—except that he will come to accept the limitations of himself as a finite being; of what his agency can extend to the client and how; and of his hard-won conviction that no one, not even he, can *know* another human being. He becomes a helper who is like the scientist in the respect that he can establish the conditions (of which he is one) within the helping process and this agency, and must await the outcome that he can neither predict nor force. And, like many scientists, too, he needs belief.

Toward this helper and away from him, the client will move in the process of growth and change which takes him from unfreedom to freedom, to action, to responsibility for his part in the problems he brought. With the helper and the agency he represents, the client will tussle as he strives in this way and in that to find solutions and to invent explanations. Upon the helper will be placed the client's projections, those parts of the self the client wants to discard or those parts he cannot claim. He will be the one asked to make things right, to relieve the sufferer from responsibilities he shuns or assigns to those in his social life whose pressures he feels. From him will be sought causes for the client's predicament and specific directions as to what is the best thing to do. With him, no matter what the client's content in present problem and life experiences may be, is the engagement in human relationship of the seeker of help and his "other," and that other is this time a professional caseworker.

Being human as well as professional, the caseworker does not act as a sounding board, as some students are wont to say when they begin to feel their difference from the person they are helping. He is not at his desk to listen as any good friend might. He responds with that very inner and contained self he has for so long been growing. The reality of his function and of his agency's structures are part of that self as is the reality of his own spontaneous expression, which in immediacy of feeling meets the feeling of his client. Real are his expectations, though not always put into words, that the client be the man he can be, that he take the responsibility for his own actions, small as they may be at first. Real, too, is his consideration for all the client brings to him and for each word he says. Real are his compassion and his caring for his particular individual, not simply mankind in general. All this and so much more make up the reality that is the caseworker.

Then that time comes when the client, with his increasing sense of his own responsibility for his own life, sees ahead of him escape from his predicament only if help is such that he can be told what to do and where to go, now at the moment. He pushes with his aroused strength against the helper who whatever he may offer does not give him what he wants. To the client, the helping person is the obstacle in his way while at the same time holding the key to the problem. To the client, it is the helper who must be defeated.

This force directed against him with such negative power, or, sometimes with such negative, sweet unwillingness, the helper feels directly upon himself. He alone is the one who can sense the crisis of the moment and prevent its dissipation into the lure of the client to distract him. He alone is the one who can take into himself, integrate into one single reality, all of the aspects of reality he has been holding for this now strong and angry individual. Unless he can become at this all important time the single reality, both he and the client will be lost in the limbo of superficialities, in other words, in failure. Only he is able to integrate function, structure, caring, will, impulse, intellect all into the one human being who is now only and singly: the helper.

If he can be just this, the helper, who has no more to offer than has been offered, who is there as he has been in all the seeker has experienced thus far, he has given to his client not freedom but the single, unchangeable, immovable reality in relation to which the client can if he will, find himself anew. The client now has come alone to the acute pain of retracting his vaunted pride in the expression of inner need—plainly and simply—need.

Such expression feels total, as if he will desert his independent self. The helper can only wait; he does not give the "answer," which would be scorned if he did. Yet the waiting is difficult to bear. What sustains him at this moment is his belief in his client's inner direction toward growth, belief in his function, belief in his skill, belief in the process that holds for this man the true healing that comes from himself, the client. But belief even backed with experience after experience, gives no assurance, no right to predict, that each future experience will be the same. It might be.

This, then, is the caseworker the student will become some day after he is no longer a student. This is the helper he has wanted to be who offers the client a growth-inducing experience through the casework process. This is the caseworker he begins to become from the first day in his social work school. And in his own learning, he will need to live this same underlying process in his relationship to those who will teach him. He needs to live it not simply to be able to say, "I, too, have experienced the process," but because he is a human being and cannot escape it. What he could escape as a client and not as a person who will one day present himself as ready to help others is his own awareness of the process while he is in the midst of it.

Should it be so that the human being pushes through the maze of external realities ever to seek a singleness in the face of which he can find his own truth and act to choose his own direction, the human being who is the student of a professional school has no singleness in the split learning structure that is his. As has been mentioned, this learning structure is not just split in two, but into fragments. There are many teachers, as many as six for the student on campus, in addition to the supervisor in agency.

In the chapters ahead we shall see how one school has tackled the problem of multiple learning in the academic courses and the problem of offering the student a fusion of school and agency as the single reality he needs for choice to learn to become the social caseworker.

PART TWO

THEORY AND PRACTICE IN
PROCESS

4

BEGINNING ON CAMPUS

Writing the first words purporting to describe practice makes apparent the impossibility of separating fact from feeling, theory from practice. Work over a period of more than four decades has gone into the creation of a school of social work and the theory that supports it, work performed by many individuals whose contributions cannot here be singled out one from the other. Within those decades, the years from 1950 to the present have been and are being devoted by those individuals to the development of a Block Plan structure and to the teaching within it. The structures that have been erected for this school are in no one's mind the best that could be, nor are they the only structures wherein a process of concurrence, fusion, and choice might evolve. The practice and the theory together make in living operation one school of social work, the school at the University of North Carolina. Imperfect and perfectible, its doors open, its spokesman now takes responsibility for this presentation of those parts of the school pertinent to the theme of this essay.

A concurrent relationship of school and agency we might say begins before the student reaches the campus. The first term of the first year, or of the second year, for that matter,

could not get under way if an agreement is not reached
between school and agency. A representative of the school
talks with a representative of the agency in an administrative
conference in regard to student placement, the school's
standards for supervision, practical requirements for the
undertaking of practice instruction of students, the agency's
questions about school participation, and the likeness or not
of the school's and agency's goals and philosophies of social
work. The school and agency are contemporary, and they
reach a first agreement in this start toward concurrence.

Where does the student's process begin?

When we consider the two-pronged dilemma of the
academic and professional expectations that are upon the
student, we might say that it begins for him when he has
the first hint in the application process. Even before he sub-
mits his application, he has to say tentatively at least that he
can and will meet these expectations and become a student
of academic work on the campus and of actual helping in the
agency. One young man in a preliminary interview with a
member of the admissions committee said what we might
infer others often feel before they take the step into formal
application.

"People like me," he said, "and like to talk with me. I
think I could help them . . . but I went to college on an
athletic scholarship and I don't know about my grades. . . ."

Before he had asked for an application form, he had had
to examine his dual qualifications. A young woman applicant
who had more than likely posed this same question to herself
and who followed through to application, gives evidence in
the application interview of the dilemma for her. The interviewer records:

After I let her know that all her application material was in
and quite acceptable, she plunged in to telling me that she was
quite surprised at herself for being in social work. She really has
put no conscious effort into it. Things just happened. She

began in secretarial work in college because her father is practical and thought she should be able to earn a living—then when she decided that she didn't want that and changed to sociology he had said that might be good as in view of her attitude about family illness, she needed to have more compassion. Maybe he didn't use those words but that was what he meant. She wrote "casework" for her career on a questionnaire in her junior year at college because it was easiest.

This young applicant apparently convinced herself that the practical career with its reason and its logic, she could have had but had cast it away; that the helping career with its feeling and its compassion, she had doubts about for the person she was. In the interview she began to learn that to become a caseworker, or even an accepted applicant, she could not remain so split and helpless in the hands of fate.

To make this discovery through self-generation is a difficult if not impossible task. The applicant needs the interviewer, and from our point of view the interviewer needs to know from experience whether the applicant can make such a discovery. For both, one test of whether an applicant gives indication of being able to learn in this difficult setting should come in the application interview.

One tall, fine-looking young man came to his interview and sat stiffly, formally, without expression. Even when he learned that his application material with transcripts, references, and his own statement was acceptable, his frozen face changed not a whit. The interviewer recorded:

Mr. W began stiffly to tell me of his interest in social work and of his feeling of readiness for further study. Rather as though he were reciting a lesson he told me about his adolescent experiences and how he had come through a period of maladjustment. He is thankful and wants to help others. In a stiff recital, he told of his desire for social work training, pausing once in a while as though to remind himself of his preconceived sentences. His very youthful face was turned from me and set.

I said here that it seemed as though he were working very hard, and I could understand that as this was an important interview, but it was as though he were, in a way, making a speech to me.

Mr. W's response was immediate. He shifted in his chair, smiled broadly and said that was just what he was doing. To tell the truth he has a real fear of graduate school training and yet he does want to come. From here on, Mr. W was much more relaxed and increasingly related.

With the interviewer's seemingly simple remark, this young man elected to release himself from his tight fear, revealing himself as spontaneous and ready to become warmly related to this strange interviewer who had represented to him at first only the awesome requirements of the graduate school.

The instant response in feeling when the self has been touched through the content of its efforts to convince or to refuse to be convinced, makes evident, it would seem, the instant interacting of intellect and emotion. The instant response has thinking in it and yet is too fast to be thought out; it has feeling in it, yet it is contained and communicable; it has will in it, yet the rigid control is gone; it moves out of impulse and yet has none of the onrushing of raw impulse. Perhaps this response, unpretentious as it may appear in a single interview, is the feeling, thoughtful act of will rising from the life impulse in response to the other person's touch upon him through the vagaries and varieties of content, with caring. For this young man, in his instant response he may have found, in microcosm, and without being aware of it, a resolution to the split learning experience he would encounter later as a student.

The first term gets under way. The applicant, now a student, arrives on campus in September. He has met the school through his application interview and later through interviews or correspondence about his field work placement to which he will report in late November.

Over the years, a change has taken place in this structure of the placement of first-year students. Many, if not all, schools surely must know something of the struggles to find a way to assign placements that are practicable for the school and educationally sound for the student. At the North Carolina school, we tried many ways before coming to the plan that is at present in operation. Without going into the details, the plan is that of notifying the accepted applicant of his particular placement (assured by the school's administrative clearance with agency) as soon after his acceptance as possible, often in the spring preceding his first year. By the time applications have been accepted to the limit of our school's capacity, most of the incoming students have confirmed their placements and, by the opening of the school in the fall, all of the first-year class-members are settled as far as their field placement is concerned. The fall term, which had heretofore been spent by faculty and student on the arduous matter of placement, heightened by the urgency of the student to secure the right one quickly, is now relieved of at least this complication.

The first-year student arrives on campus and soon meets classes with six professors, each with a different subject and a different expectation of him. These courses, similar to ones taught in most schools of social work under perhaps other titles or in other configurations, include group process, research, medical information, child welfare, public welfare, casework, and human growth and development. At this writing, the seven courses are taught by six professors.

Often the faculty has thought of the variety the student is asked to carry, assimilate, and learn, and has wondered whether there can be a way to bring this varying content together into a cohesive and related whole. But how? Practically, it would be a staggering problem provided that we thought the integration of content by the school makes for integration of learning by the student. We have considered, on the other hand, that the university system of this country offers the student the opportunity to meet and to learn from many professors from their special fields and with their unique and personal approaches. The social work student may need this opportunity no less than other students. In fact, some social work students may need this impact with difference more than other students; and some social work students may need it more than other social work students. To endeavor to remove difference, except for the basic philosophy of the school, seemed not to be the simple answer to the student's integration in learning.

Although this thinking on the part of the faculty in no way precludes its examination of the curriculum nor the institution of changes in it, the faculty did, through creative work in the group, bring into being an advisory system which, as it has unfolded over the years, has led to the conviction that the unity represented by an adviser presents the school as a whole to the student as the effort to integrate content might not. Each student has as his faculty adviser his casework teacher (or the teacher of the process course in whatever concentration he elects, such as administration or, should it become organized, group work) during the campus terms and also during the field work term. In this way, as far as the academic work is concerned, the student does have a single individual who at critical points can represent the school for him; and the multiplicity is removed functionally, though momentarily, when singleness is needed.

In bringing this advisory plan into being, the faculty had adjustments to make. There were those who, each with a great interest in and concern for students in the advisory relationship, had to be willing to forgo the joy—and the responsibility and hard work—of being advisers to students. The casework teachers had to be willing to take upon themselves a larger share of responsibility and to move out into unknown paths. Each group willingly acceded to what all considered an orderly way of working and a potential for more effective education.

The new first-year student meets with his adviser soon after he arrives on campus, and it is with him that he begins the process of relationship which continues until June. This same plan is in effect for the second-year students when they return to school after a summer recess following their first year. The adviser in his functional capacity, which relates him to school and to agency, carries through this first term the intimation for the student of the split in his learning and of the practice that is to come. He carries with him too, and the student knows it, the actual connection that has been made with the agency the student has confirmed is to be his.

For the immediate present of the campus term, the adviser becomes also the casework teacher who has the task of teaching the group. The student cannot sit and wait for field work or even simply spend these weeks getting ready for it; he has work to do in learning of casework here and now. This first-year course in casework is probably one of the most difficult of courses to teach. In ten weeks, with only the promise of practice before them, the clients existing only in their projections, the student must learn something of what casework entails. The student who has never been inside a social agency or the student who has been working for years has to be introduced to what is meant by taking and giving help, by agency function and structure, by professional relationships, and by the simple ethics of being a caseworker.

Like any other teacher of casework, the teacher of the casework course on the Block Plan comes to realize that in a classroom where casework is taught with the use of bought or borrowed or live case material, case material of last week or of yesterday can be deadly dull. The recency of the case, recorded and mimeographed, does not guarantee life for the classroom. A student's own recent case being discussed in class does not necessarily inspirit the discussion. The exchange of yesterday's experience from student to student can be as empty as the exchange of last year's. If there is no life in the people participating in the class, there is no life. Beneath the content, whatever it may be, runs the relationship that makes for the life of the classroom learning. The Block Plan teacher can be as creative as he has it in him to be within the limitations of the class, himself, and his subject right up to the inevitable stopping place, practice in the social agency.

On the other hand, the Block Plan teacher cannot assume that the lack of current casework experience has no bearing upon the teaching or the learning. He must assume, rather, that it has a fundamental bearing. What is missing is the learning of a skill in practice in an agency—for the duration of the campus term. As far as the casework class is concerned, the Block Plan student is as immersed or can be as immersed in the learning process as any Concurrent Plan student who, like him, cannot learn a skill in the classroom. To let the learning of practice (for it cannot be a skill as yet) remain in the future, or for some students in the past, and to provide a learning in the present is one pedagogical distinction and problem of the Block Plan.

Another course indirectly and vitally connected with the student's agency experience presents in two terms of the first year and one term in the second year the psychological background for all the casework taught in the school. This course and the casework course compose the core of the practice curriculum on campus. It is the course that is, although the student may not always realize it, for him to use for himself as he learns so intensely in these two courses and the other five and is also expected to change and to grow. Social Work 209, "Psychological Backgrounds for the Helping Professions," is the course that of all in this busy fall term incurs the sharpest reaction from the student. It has to do with himself and is the truly new in the graduate school he has chosen.

From the school's files is taken this notation from a student's record:

Miss Q began this course with a burst of enthusiasm and then, though writing good short papers, did a mediocre term paper which did not seem even up to her chatty ability. She settled into a kind of negative carping in class. When I saw Miss Q in conference, she fought me up and down, "giving me the benefit of the doubt" she said, adding, however, that she had no feeling one way or the other! I held her to the fact that she was not learning in this class, the methods of which were not going to be changed for her. Toward the end of the hour, she sat quietly and then she burst out: "But it's all so new!" From then on Miss Q was more related, full of feeling, and she said, with great wonder, that she did not need to have the reasons she had been pushing so hard for....

What was so new to the student? Was it simply the content of this psychological backgrounds course, so new and different and difficult to learn, or was it the expectation of a learning that was more fundamental than the mastery of content?

Some social work educators who believe that the social work student should reach a degree of self-awareness in order to become a caseworker are of the opinion that such self-awareness can be achieved only in the field work experience. We have come to believe differently and have seen it evidenced among the students year after year that their awareness of self is very much present as it was for Miss Q during the campus term. Although we have the expectation of such self-awareness beginning on campus and make it possible for the student to meet these expectations if he can, such learning in immediate awareness of self is not entirely new.

Great teachers of the past have brought to their students, in addition to the content to which they have been devoted as teachers and to which they have devoted their lives, two special functions, in Gilbert Highet's use of the term.[1] One of these functions, he says, is that they make a bridge between the school and the world; the other is that they make a bridge between maturity and youth. In other words, they make themselves relevant. Possessing knowledge of their subject, they also possess the living of life; possessing years chronologically, they possess also youth. As long as their teaching is out of this relevance, the student may learn both contentually and experientially with awareness even in the most unlikely of subjects. Many a student knows of entering the classroom or lecture hall grumpily and sullenly, chafing at the requirement to attend, and of leaving transported in the excitement of intellectual attainment through a living experience with a vital teacher. To universities, the experiential side of learning is not new.

What may be new is that a school of social work on the Block Plan may expect such learning of its students, as through a great teacher, for example, and not let it come about merely by chance. Yet in the North Carolina school, we do not see the course in psychological backgrounds as having for its purpose the student's achievement of self-awareness. The purpose is for the student to learn the psychological content that in the first term of first year includes in part: will, impulse, projection, identification, difference. This content the student is expected to learn. We develop the course, however, out of the conviction that psychological concepts are not learned through an exchange of content and opinion, that they are rooted in the very human self of each student.

When the student reads about the soldier preparing for

1. Gilbert Highet, *The Art of Teaching* (New York: Vintage Book, 1959), pp. 49-53.

battle or even the rat running the maze, he is apt to ask himself, "How is it, how would it be, for me?" He is apt also not to ask the question aloud. Rather than to deny that the student does direct psychological content to himself where it can churn around, the teaching of this course anticipates the churning around in his own immediate process. In the discussion of will, for example, the student projecting his own will upon the fictional characters of the reading assignment, speaks in class about will without at first knowing that it is of his own will he speaks. That the student will push against the teacher in class as well as in conference is expected by the teacher, and the student learns to be responsible for it. It may not be easy on the teacher but there is life in the campus term. And the process, as time and teaching and learning in all courses go on, moves from the negative to the warm relatedness of learning in identification.

At the close of her two years in school, Miss Q wrote a final paper mentioning this first-year experience:

That this yielding of the own negative will should be resisted seems natural to me now. In this deep impact felt with difference, a very vulnerable part of the self had been touched. Much of the false self had been stripped of its veneer and I did, indeed, have to admit need of the other. For me, this impact with difference carried deep meaning. It was the point at which I chose to enter the School of Social Work and to begin to take help to learn to be a caseworker. I know for myself that this impact with the difference of the helper was necessary before my process of learning could get underway.

Miss Q learned with self-awareness. A criticism directed toward such teaching might be that the student would learn only from his own psychology. This is a danger. But when self-awareness and self-knowledge are clearly differentiated, the danger may be avoided. A psychology taught for the student to gain knowledge of the causative factors of his own past as interpreted by himself and his teacher might result in his making universal his own psychology. To become aware of himself in immediate experience and to learn as his classmates, too, are learning, relieves the strain of the highly personal and irremediable and of trying to build the universal out of the particular. He finds a sense of human likeness, even in difference. The connection of concept and experience the student makes for himself.

As a student said in her final casework paper:

In courses the helping process could have been presented, lectured on and studied as removed from our experience and this is the way it would have remained. We could have talked about ambivalence, strivings of the will, beginnings, impact, separations, and endings in relation to something outside ourselves and it would have stayed there—outside the realm of understanding which could not be used in relationship to clients. Reading about impact with difference is one thing—feeling it is quite another.

It was not just "she" who had learned but "we" who had learned the concepts as content and experience and who had reached a self-awareness in this first term of the first year before they had, some of them, ever been in a social agency.

During the last week of the fall term, the first-year student has an opportunity to meet the supervisors who come to Chapel Hill for the supervisors' meeting. We have found this to be a momentous day. An appointment is arranged for the student to have a brief talk with his own supervisor, who in a week or ten days will be helping him to begin in his actual work with troubled people. This meeting has taken its place as a part of the student's ending with the school for the first campus term as well as an introduction to the field practice to come. The essentiality of this meeting of supervisors to them, many of whom are supervising for the first time with the school, has been recognized in schools other than ours. Some might question the student's introduction to agency before he is there, but had not our conviction grown from practice, it would be less than polite for the supervisor to be on campus and not meet his student!

Just before Thanksgiving, the first-year students leave for agencies that may be located at Savannah, Georgia, or Wilmington, Delaware, or some place between.

The second-year students by this time are already in their field placements and have been since early in September, as we shall see later. They arrived in July on campus for a six-week term, met with their adviser, and began with him in the casework course. At this writing, the summer curriculum consists of the casework course, a course in community organization, and the third term of the psychological backgrounds course. This summer curriculum has undergone considerable change through the years for one reason or another. As yet there has not been enough experience with this present plan to mention here. The one experience we can stand by for the students is that the importance of the summer has been held for them through the adviser-teacher and the casework course.

Like the teacher of the first-year casework course, the second-year teacher faces a class looking forward to its field work and, for all of the class members, also glancing backward. They have not been in the field practice since March. Sometimes, we are asked whether it would not be better to arrange, as some Block Plan schools do, to have the students go directly to their placements without a preliminary second-year campus term. Our response has been, on the basis of our experience with this plan and with our teachers who have become advisers to students in the field having had no previous relationship with them, that for learning in both class and field of the depth we have come to expect, the student needs to begin his year's work in the educational institution and to start his field work with a relationship established on campus.

In the summer, the students of the casework class discuss cases that are strange to them all. Quite soon in the discussion, the student finds an identification with the client who is coming to an agency for help: an identification with the way he presents himself, his problems, and the impact he meets. By the time the class has read and is discussing a case in which the client is adamantly refusing the caseworker's offer of help, this situation seems more real and immediate than any case the student himself may have carried in the past. The class, each individual member of it, becomes identified with the client in her refusal and resentful of the will of the worker which is often placed in projection upon the teacher.

When the class discovers that the client must leave the agency unbowed and also unhelped and must struggle alone with a tremendous problem, the class acknowledges that there is relief in resting upon another and in taking help from another. A shift in identification comes about as the class begins to realize that the helping process can be warm and caring and that the professional person is someone the student caseworkers can want to be like. During the class term, when this live relationship is moving beneath the content and the class is learning casework concepts, meeting reading assignments, and writing papers in the tradition of the university, the learning of the helping process has been immediate for each student.

A student writing a casework paper at the close of the summer term said in introduction:

I feel that giving and taking help are parts of living which each of us experiences almost "naturally." By referring to the helping process, I mean the whole helping process, and this, as I see it, is not remote and distant from day to day involvement with life and help, but it is a different and specific involvement about which I am seeking to deepen my understanding. . . .

I feel that I am risking making an outline and calling it the helping process. An outline will not do though because as I see it, help is experienced through a process, and processes can be outlined; but in the helping process, two individual selves are involved and to me this means that each and every process has to be new and different.

Out of her fresh present learning, this student writes of the helping process as a day-by-day process, not remote from life, universal and yet unique. She wants to deepen her understanding as she writes her paper and finds the clichés or the "outline" of the process devoid of the living quality of relationship. She wants to bring together the logic of an outline with the illogic of human beings; and although it is unlikely that she succeeded, she could not have chosen this subject had she not been experiencing a learning that had in it the stuff of life itself.

By the end of the summer term, the student is eager to move away from the campus and on to the opportunity to become himself a caseworker. To his agency placement, the student takes this beginning in second year, a learning that has been both contentual and experiential. Another student writing in a term paper at the close of her second year and thinking back to the summer term said: "The helping process, it seems to me as a student in the summer, was not one in which I was consciously aware of the process; but as I moved into the field placement and became the caseworker, a new awareness of the process came to me. This now seems to me to have arisen from my own experience in using help in the School setting. Then as I moved along in field placement I became more aware of my being involved in the process . . . it is more a part of this encounter becoming a natural part of oneself. . . . "

The class finishes the summer term and has ahead the months in the field work agency and a return to the campus for the final spring term. Although usually there have been two individual conferences with each student held by the teacher-adviser during the summer, the class finishes as a unit before its members scatter to the several states. The ending of the term is an ending with a class that remains a class even though each student will necessarily have an individual relation with the adviser in the months to come.

The student who, it is hoped, has come through at the close of the campus term with an integration of himself, of his learning of content, and of experience at one with the given inner forces of his nature, now moves to agency. The two-pronged problem of the academic and the professional has become part of the single individual insofar as it can be in the single institution of learning. He moves on to the expectation that he will be the university's student in the agency; he moves on to a new split in his learning. The responsibility of the adviser and the supervisor who is awaiting the student's arrival seems clear to us—to bring together the two parts into one whole, even if only momentarily at one point of time and in one place, for the student to meet as the single reality and choose, or refuse, to learn.

5

POINT OF CONCURRENCE

The concurrent relationship between adviser and supervisor begins in their first meeting in conference. This meeting takes place, for the North Carolina school and its agencies, about a week before field work begins in the first year, as we have mentioned, and about a week following the start of field work in the second year. The conferences are held individually with each supervisor in conjunction with a general meeting for supervisors of the particular class. In the general meeting, our concern has been with the beginning of the process for all students and the structure of the school which pertains to school and agency through the field work term. In the individual conference, the focus of adviser and supervisor is the student who will be coming to the agency or who has just arrived.

The supervisor who is beginning his supervisory experience for the first time or for the tenth is usually eager to tell the adviser about the agency, the selection of cases, and the way the student may begin or has begun. The adviser finds himself coming to the end of what he and his colleagues can offer the student for the present. The student needs practice. In this conference, the adviser says to the supervisor, in effect or in actual words, "You are the supervisor. Even though you may have been my student just two years ago, you are the supervisor from your agency. I cannot do my work without you." This statement or this inner declaration sounds like one of yielding, of going with the inevitable by choice, not by submission; a yielding not to the other person, but of the own will to its own inevitable limits and its own need. The achieving of such a yielding is not easy for an adviser who is usually a person of years of experience, considerable knowledge, a well-developed will, and a charge to be responsible for the student's learning.

The supervisor is not so far along in the beginning of the concurrent relationship by the end of this day as is the adviser. Nor could he be.

For all of the discussions in general meeting and conference, for all of his lack of specific knowledge about the school or its working relation to the agency, even for his own newness to the supervisory job and his desire to learn what he can on this day, the supervisor has not yet felt a need for school or adviser. Many supervisors, I am sure, will firmly disagree, saying that supervisors need the agency's help before they begin their supervision of the student or surely on the first day or after a week. They do need assistance, and the school tries to give them that assistance through meeting and conference. But they may agree, after they have experienced the full process, that the cry for help arising from inner need does not come quickly, and on this day the supervisor could not possibly be at that point. He has not yet reached the limit of his own teaching of the student, but when he does his need will be acute.

The supervisor has the difficult job of teaching the practice of social casework to a student who has become a student of the university during the campus term and who has yet to become a student in the agency. It will take time for this transformation to come about for both student and supervisor, and the school knows it. As often as the supervisor may have begun with students and seen them past the turning point where they can be students in the agency, he still in all likelihood wants to believe that this new student will be different from the others. Unique as each student is in his pattern of meeting with his outside world, and each supervisor, too, neither can overcome the human process of relationship into which they are entering with such high hopes. The adviser who must rely upon the supervisor to carry the teaching of practice cannot lift a finger to make the situation other than it is. He and the school however, can and do anticipate the time when both supervisor and student will reach the point of not being able to go on alone and will need them.

The school establishes a structure of advisory visits to student and supervisor at the agency.

The setting of structure in a school of social work is not a simple matter administratively or educationally, according to our experience. What is the optimum time span for the academic terms? for the field work terms? How can these time spans be fitted into the university calendar? If changes must be made—and they have been made several times in our school—what effect will they have upon the graduate school's board on down to the youngest first-year student? And when the timing sequence has been established, how often can and should the faculty visit agency and student? In relation to what events should the visits be planned? These questions peculiar to the Block Plan are raised by each Block Plan school, without doubt, and no attempt shall be made here to answer them. They do hint at the breadth and depth of the problems of structure. They do hint also at the constant evaluation and re-evaluation that must take place within a school's faculty and never with a sense of finality.

The time structure at the University of North Carolina

School of Social Work includes at present three and three-quarter months of full-time field-practice in the first year and five and one-half months of full-time practice in the second year. The first year academic and practice terms are completed in the nine-month university school year. The second year has an additional six-week summer term preceding the regular school year. In both years, the adviser visits the agency twice.

The faculty never cease to be amazed at what the students accomplish in the short time they have to make the major change of locale from campus to agency. The student completes his campus term with a sense of learning and an eagerness to be about the business of helping people. He makes plans for moving to another city, packs, finds a place to live, may have a few days of vacation, and reports at the agency on the date set. These activities are completed in a week or ten days in second year and even less in first year. But completed they are, and well.

During the first-year field work term, the adviser travels to each agency before or just after Christmas and again in late January or early February. In order to reach all of the agencies twice in their geographically separated locations and within the brief time span, the adviser must visit some students in their early beginnings before they have had time to stub their toes or before the supervisor has felt any need for the school in helping carry through this difficult job. For others in the first visit after Christmas, and for all by the second visit, the sense of crisis has appeared; and the choice to learn, and with it the choice whether to remain in school and in the field of social work, has been made before the students return to campus in March.

Beginning with the year 1963-64, this plan for advisory visits to first-year students in the field will be modified. The faculty have reviewed the present plan and decided to institute, instead, a single advisory visit to be made during the sixth, seventh, or eighth week of the student's field work term. This timing is anticipated to meet the crisis in learning and the supervisor's need for the adviser's help. A second visit can, of course, be made if necessary. This structural change will bring with it new problems as yet unforeseen, but it promises a closer relatedness to the student's actual learning process. The experience of the timing of the first advisory visit in the second-year program provides some practical guides for this new first-year plan. Should the three and three-quarter months first-year field work term, which is quite short, be extended, it is possible that two advisory visits would be resumed.

For the second-year field work term, with its longer time span, the advisory visits can be more leisurely spaced. The students begin field work in early September, and we have found that agency visits made in September or even early October have been too soon. The student is still not past the stage of finding himself in relation to the external necessities of the new job and has not yet admitted to any inadequacy in his ability to help clients. The first visit coming in November has been usually too late. The student and the supervisor have had to wait too long alone and in need of the adviser. There are about three weeks or so in October when visits to agencies seem to us to be optimum for both student and supervisor. It has proved possible for the faculty adviser to visit all his students and agencies in those weeks in October, even returning to Chapel Hill each week to teach another class, provided that the locations of the field work agencies are somewhat concentrated, the distances limited, and the number of students fifteen or less. In January, a second visit is made, some of the details of which will be mentioned in a later chapter.

Although the structure of time and of timing the advisory visits has to be different in the first and second years and although the students are, of course, at different

levels in their development, the underlying process of the
student's learning through the relationship with the school
and agency remains the same for all. Time and again we see
the students, each in his own unique pattern, whether in first
or second year, moving along the same route to learning.
Where the structure differs between the two years, it will
need to be introduced into our discussion here; the student's
process that evolves within the structure and always in
relation to an adviser and a supervisor, we assume to be, as
has been said earlier, the human process of change and
growth.

The adequacy with which the student often begins his
field work term is not so surprising to find in the second-
year student as in the first, and yet it is so for both. The
fear of setting forth on a new and most important project is
present with him, of course, but in the hurried week of
preparations and in the relief of having arrived at all, the
fear is often well in hand. Not fear but will is in charge of
the student. The first-year student, who has never worked
in an agency before the week he is just concluding, may say
to his supervisor with as much vehemence as the second-year
student did some months earlier: "But I ought to know how
to do it. I learned it in school!"

One supervisor wrote in her mid-term evaluation: "Miss
A's start with the agency was as if she were a newly
engaged worker who was self-possessed and fully in com-
mand of beginning a new job.... There were moments
when I wondered whether Miss A was truly a student."
And, of course Miss A was not a student; that is, not yet a
student of the agency. She had become a student at the
university during the campus term, and she had gained
knowledge and experience that in her able way she could
put to use through her will to carry on without a supervisor.
She had not become a student of the agency in any sense of
the word except the title, nor had her classmate about whom

his supervisor had written, "Upon beginning his learning experience, Mr. B impressed me rather immediately with his very good intellectual grasp of casework concepts and principles. In our beginning conferences, he moved easily and quickly into what he felt patients and families were experiencing and feeling in asking for help. He moved into agency and work situations quickly and in an acceptable, independent and responsible way." Miss A and Mr. B had the reins of the job in their own hands and were starting their field work most competently, fear well submerged in their wills to go it alone.

Of Mr. B his supervisor wrote at mid-term: "Mr. B floundered and struggled alone in his intensity to do things right and, quoting him, 'to be all things to all people.' In interviews he was dogmatic, directing, controlling, and 'lectured'.... He projected responsibility upon me to discover with him the areas in his work which represented weaknesses. In this, he would then say he had learned and that next time, 'I know I will know what to do.'" By this time Mr. B evidently was not learning, and he had heard about it from his supervisor. But the "I will know what to do" is still his effort to teach himself. Mr. C's supervisor, writing in the mid-term, too, was having an experience with Mr. C similar to that of Mr. B's supervisor with Mr. B. He noted that Mr. C "controlled the situation by letting me know he had a difficult time in his last field work placement as well as at school, was aware of his problems, and was working on them, indicating that he was asking me for no further help with them. At the same time I felt he was expecting a great deal of me, but leaving the responsibility for giving him what he needed entirely up to me."

These students and many others say, in effect, that the supervisor should carry all of the responsibility and at another time that they, the students, must carry it all. They say that if they are only told what to do, they will do it. In any case, they do not want to be touched. Survive they might alone; but reaching the fulfillment in learning and in helping which they held for themselves and felt being held for them by school and agency, they begin to discover, has its problems. As long as the student is insisting upon learning only on his own terms, and the agency's client is not being helped except with superficial adequacy, the supervisor cannot long recognize newness as an excuse for lack of helpfulness.

What has been taking place between student and supervisor is a clash of wills. The supervisor who has been charged with teaching the student—in fact, requiring of him a certain mode of behavior in the agency—is restricting the student's natural impulse to go out and "help." As kind as the supervisor tries to be, he cannot rid himself of what he is: the supervisor charged with this student's change in order to learn. The student, controlled and able as he might be, cannot rid himself of the human distaste for having someone try to change him even into what he is asking to become. Nor can he rid himself easily of the human pride that insists that he already knows how to act as a caseworker in an agency and that if he does not, he can figure it out. This struggle of wills cannot be resolved in agency only, despite the most skillful supervision or supervisory help from the agency to the supervisor. Always there is the gap for the student, and he knows it: this agency is not the school.

During these early weeks, the student keeps the school as a silent partner at his side. The second-year student, who has lived through field work and adviser's visits before and who has come to an awareness of self in that earlier process, enters field work with the words of wanting help on his tongue but the determination to show he can do without it in his will and every act. He does not need an agency teacher when his teachers, as he found in his hard work on campus, are back at the university.

One student wrote in a term paper at the close of the school year:

I went into this new process with somewhat the same resistance as I had possessed at the beginning of school. I had allowed one person in . . . there was no need to allow my supervisor any part of me. All I wanted from my supervisor were answers to my questions. There was no need to put myself into another relationship. I did not need anything from my supervisor. . . . As I endeavored to keep this barrier between my supervisor and myself, I soon found that I was not accomplishing very much. When my work day came to an end, I was completely exhausted. Again I was carrying all the burdens on my own shoulders. Something was wrong; I could not be in the process alone. I had to share myself if I wished help. Again my resistance was hurdled by my adviser and supervisor. . . .

With the hope that this young man, now a supervisor himself, has learned that his resistance was not hurdled by others but lowered through his own action, it is nevertheless possible to feel from his writing the re-creation of those days of trying to maintain the self alone and intact while pushing forward to meet the expectations of his school and the potential and direction that were his own. There is also here the growing awareness that things are not quite as they should be and that maybe, down beneath his independence, he desires someone to help carry this burden for him.

Part of the supervisor's strength in these first weeks may well be directed against the school and the adviser. It is not easy to supervise a student who will not learn, no matter whether he exhibits active resistance or an impressive ability and control, both of which keep the supervisor safely out of reach. It is not easy to have to admit an inability to complete a job. Hoping still to be able to do it alone, the supervisor may work with increasing determination to help

Mr. B or Mr. C; he may do nothing to upset the poise of Miss A; or, if he has previously experienced advisory visits, he may wait for the adviser to come. The supervisor, too, is engaged in a process that he cannot see through to completion alone.

The definite promise of an advisory visit, we believe, offers both student and supervisor a structure to which they can hold during the beginning. The vague promise of a visit when needed would be unlikely to give much firmness to either. The adviser cannot be long unaware that he and the school are needed. He comes for the first visit to an agency where student and supervisor, one personally and one functionally, have been trying each in his own way to change the other and to do the job alone.

Hundreds of miles from the campus, the adviser may find himself seated in an office requisitioned for his use: the supervisor's office, a storeroom, a doctor's examining room, a waiting room, a worker's office, an executive's office. Once in a while, in the rare agency with no space problem, he might have the use for the day of an unoccupied, furnished office where he can have conferences with both supervisor and student. The Block Plan adviser, especially one who has had experience as adviser on the Concurrent Plan, may covet the comfort of remaining in his own office on campus and having the supervisor and student meet him there.

Wherever he has his office on the day of the visit, the adviser has an important job to do and a limited time in which to do it. The time structure for conferences does vary from school to school. We have usually, since undertaking the Block Plan structure, scheduled one hour with the supervisor, one hour with the student, and then a brief conference again with the supervisor. This order or this timing may be varied by individual advisers, but on the Block Plan, the fact remains that a limited time highlights the necessity for the adviser to make every minute count. When he leaves, he will once again be hundreds of miles away.

In this first agency visit, the adviser and the supervisor begin their second conference in the concurrent process. They have corresponded; the student has written an assignment paper and had a response. Their coming together now is in some ways like another beginning and in other ways very much like a step in continuation of an ongoing relationship. The supervisor who has had the awesome responsibility for the student's progress to date and who has until now considered it his duty that the student learn, as indeed it is, may now feel the relief of the adviser's presence. For all his efforts to present the school with an exceptional student who is learning to capacity through supervision only, he has not succeeded and feels accountable to this other organization outside of his own. The adviser is aware that no supervisor can accomplish this feat alone and that although the new supervisor may have made mistakes and may not be as skillful in supervision as one day he will, he cannot do what no human could do in his position. He cannot make the agency into the school.

There can be relief for the supervisor in sharing with the adviser the student's beginning in agency. There can be pride and hope in a job well done yet unfinished; concern for failure to reach his own expectations; blame for the student in his negative perversity; all these, shared with the adviser, may bring relief to the supervisor and a change in his feeling about himself and his job as supervisor of students. Or the supervisor may still try to prove himself to the adviser, still try to maintain that the student has taken or that he cannot take the necessary steps in learning, and without saying so directly, still try to overcome the school. Supervisors may not all be at the same place in the concurrent process. The adviser needs to realize that each supervisor is engaging in the process and that the student's very livelihood in the school depends upon it.

Beneath the exchange of content, the process runs toward its immediate limit, the adviser's conference with the student, alone. The supervisor already has been informed of the fact that the adviser does not read the student's records, and that fact contributes we believe to the understanding the supervisor has at the time of the visit that the adviser will in no way take over supervisory duties with the student. Before seeing the student, however, the adviser usually tells the supervisor once more that the function of the conference is not to supervise. It is to hold the student to the agreed upon school-agency expectation for all social work students that the student shift in his attitude toward learning. The agreement between adviser and supervisor in regard to the particular student, not simply for all students, next is essential. This agreement, both general and particular, of two contemporary agencies through their representatives is a step without which concurrence can go no further.

On this day and in his conference with the adviser, the student is offered the opportunity to meet this expectation in order to become a caseworker, if he will.

One supervisor in his mid-term evaluation of the student wrote:

With the approaching time of the adviser's visit, Mr. D began to feel more of the pressure of his own feelings and fear and began what I consider to be a better learning use of supervision. He began to trust and risk some of his own dogmatic feelings with me and to struggle a little regarding case situations. Although this movement was evidenced, he continued to attempt to separate his feeling regarding supervision from his over-all work. He could risk expressing feeling to me about school and adviser and, as was later seen, could risk expressing his feeling about me and the supervisory relationship to the adviser, but only after we two had come together, could he bring these feelings to the proper place. Following the adviser's visit, I do feel that Mr. D changed in his over-all use of himself. It is now possible for him to accept his making mistakes, and to offer and take difference and criticism of his operation. . . .

It was not until "we two"—"we two" being the supervisor and adviser—had got together that Mr. D could express himself directly as a student to both. The supervisor apparently was of the opinion that Mr. D had made use of the opportunity offered him in the advisory conference and was related to learning in a newly positive way.

We might stop here and conjecture that the "getting together" of supervisor and adviser is "concurrence." "Getting together" implies contemporaneousness, agreement, and a simple mutual partnership. But does a simple mutual partnership provide the single reality we are suggesting that the student needs at this point in his process? Is it the mutual partnership that makes possible the change that this student apparently made? As far as the supervisor was concerned, it may have done so, and yet we must look further. We might wonder whether this student's change continued for the time being or was the change in growth that is irreversible. In a partnership of his school and agency, he had faced two separate institutions even though both were presented to him by his adviser; in a partnership, two forces do not become one no matter how close they may seem to be. As long as there are two forces, one from the school and one from the agency, the student can still find the gap between them—and he will. There must be a step beyond mutuality.

The first move in regard to ending the time-limited conference and breaking through the mutuality must be the adviser's. He is the one who has the appointment with the waiting student, and he is the one to speak for the school-agency. It is he who first recognizes that his relationship with the supervisor is not mutual, not collaborative, not integrative. It is he who represents an institution the primary function of which is educational; through this function he is the one who is responsible for the student's learning. He and only he can take this responsibility, and taking this responsibility on this day so special in the lives of all three engaged in the process requires hard internal work of him. Many times before, he may have arrived at this moment with other supervisors and other students, yet with each such visit he repeats the hard internal work of taking into himself what is his.

Each time, with supervisor and with student, he needs to differentiate himself from the supervisor functionally. If he can yield his will to make over or change or improve the supervisor-student relationship, he may be better able to carry through the job that is his own. Too often, I have come to believe, the adviser becomes entangled in his well-meant efforts to "help" the supervisor, that is, to make the supervisor understand the student and thus to smooth the relationship that has become ruffled between them. Valuable minutes speed by and all that is accomplished is an adviser-supervisor will struggle or, by the end of the hour, a verbal agreement. Of course, the adviser expresses himself when he, for the school, differs with some part of the supervisor's practice that affects the student adversely. Yet he is not the one who lives with the day in and day out ups and downs of the student in agency. He cannot in one hour make the supervisor over according to his desires; this is not the purpose of his visit. Once again, he must come to an inner acceptance of himself as the adviser from the school and the other as the supervisor from the agency. His responsibility is for the student's learning, in the hour of this visit, directly with him.

The supervisor has his part, too, and because of his clear functional differentiation from the adviser, he can take it.

Feeling the separateness between the two of them, the supervisor can come to terms with his own two-way pull of now wanting to continue to supervise the student to success alone and now wanting to relinquish the whole situation to the adviser or student. When the supervisor can yield his will to his own inevitable limits in a process that cannot move to consummation as long as two persons endeavor to relate simultaneously to one other person; when he can contain that will within his primary function as charged to him by the institution of helping, he may actually fulfill his supervisory function. As he temporarily gives up the teaching function that has to do with the teaching of casework practice in a certain agency, and as he becomes well aware of the adviser's acceptance of the university's teaching function as including the teaching of practice, he may be making it possible for his student to achieve the positive learning he wants so much for him. In many cases, the supervisor makes this shift, and hard internal work it is, too, and is relieved when the educational function is in the hands of the one to which it belongs. He may discover now, as never before, in this relationship with the adviser, what help from the school to him, as well as to his student, can mean.

One experienced supervisor, working for the first time with a Block Plan school, wrote in her mid-term evaluation (due about December 1) of a young man who had had his first year in her agency:

Last year, Mr. T's resistance to taking help was expressed through impatience with himself. "I know; why can't I do? Why do I have to be told that?" When he returned to the agency this year, even this expression of resistance was absent. He was remote, unreachable. He was aware of his unrelatedness but tended to put the responsibility on not feeling well (a cold), on fatigue from moving and establishing an apartment, etc. His manner was tense, he looked unhappy, his participation in conferences stilted and mechanical. I was unable to reach him at any point.

About the first week in October, he had made one gesture toward me, which we both recognized, but in the next conference, he had again withdrawn. At the time of the field adviser's visit, I felt he had reached a breaking point. The climax came at the time of the field adviser's visit.

An impasse had been reached—the student's complete refusal and the supervisor's helplessness. What can the school offer to each of them?

This supervisor could admit to this impasse as she talked in conference with the adviser on the day of his October agency visit. Despite the possible and certainly human sense of failure she may have felt at not having been able to present a fully-learning, fully-engaged student whom she had brought through to success alone, this supervisor could describe the situation with honesty and accuracy. The sense of failure recedes in the face of the stronger sense of need—the need for help. The supervisor's plea becomes a plea not for help to learn how to be a supervisor but for actual help on this day, help with this resistant and non-learning student. This plea for help, spoken or not, is a yielding of the supervisor's will to change the student and indeed, perhaps, a yielding of her will to possess her educational function. Help had arrived from the university.

The adviser who represents the school in this conference with the supervisor and who anticipates a conference with the student in just one hour must, being human, feel fear. It is he who must offer help to the supervisor with her expressed need and to the student with his resistance. The adviser, too, must yield.

Without question, the adviser can agree with the supervisor, in this present moment, that the student has not learned and is not learning. Adviser and supervisor meet at a point of agreement; they concur. The agency's representative and the school's representative concur, but they remain two separate individuals with two distinct functional forces that together they cannot make into one. The adviser with his primary educational function is the one who, in yielding his will to make the other two different so as to end their own battle, yields to take into himself the force that is the educational function of the agency. It is he who in yielding fuses the school and the agency into the single educational force, the single reality. This act of will by the adviser transforms the concurrence of adviser with supervisor into the fusion of school-agency, of theory-practice.

The supervisor who has achieved concurrence with the adviser and who has given up the struggle to go it alone can well feel the relief of resting now on the greater strength. He may well feel that help has truly arrived in answer to his call.

Into the conference with the student, Mr. W, the adviser went, possessing within himself the single reality, the fusion of school-agency. Mr. W began to explain his present situation to his adviser, who he expected would understand; he had become related to his adviser in the summer. Mr. W stated that although his supervisor criticized him for lack of engagement—and such criticism might be valid—all he needed was time and he could become fully participative. His adviser, however, was not the summer casework teacher safely removed in Chapel Hill. His adviser was not simply an understanding, comforting adviser he had hoped to see. His adviser was also the agency. Mr. W met at every turn the single fused reality of the school-agency.

For Mr. W, this discovery came with a keen sense of shock. The fusion before him allowed no loophole through which to slip in further denials, projections, avoidances. The choice was his: would he meet the single expectation of life and growth in learning from the school-agency, or would he refuse it?

Mr. W took himself to the nadir of his student experience, life or death to the work he had presumably chosen for himself. One of his classmates wrote of her own experience in such a moment and expressed what Mr. W might well have said: "The turning point in my beginning experience came when my adviser visited me in the agency." She described how she had told the adviser everything was fine and that, despite the adviser's saying that she had more to do, she insisted that everything was being done. "I felt as if everything was closing in on me," she continued in her paper, "Then, with deep feeling, there was a sudden realization that I had been resisting taking any help from my supervisor.... I had tried to do it all alone." Much as the adviser wanted to say the word to relieve her or Mr. W of the tension and loneliness, he had no word to say. He could give no answers to questions, no directions as to what to do next, both of which aids the student pressed for. There are no answers and no directions to satisfy the student in his predicament. Through himself and the supervisor, the adviser has extended all that he has to extend up to this stark moment. He simply has no further resource; he *is* the final resource, the single reality. He cannot bridge the gap between himself and the student; he can only be what he is, for the student, life and growth in learning. The student himself can choose whether he wants to take it or refuse it.

The moment is without content. Truth does not lie in words. The student presses now against this single unmoving reality and finds truth for himself. When he feels the outer reality to be no longer strange and external, in a lonely instant, he has bridged the gap and admitted this outer reality into his deepest self where truth resides. Whether the flood of feeling follows the breaking through of the hard core of resistance, or whether the hard core of resistance breaks through when the flood of feeling comes in recognition of inner truth, may be hard to say. The student's wanting of union, denied for these weeks, is at last expressed when he yields his negative will and gives up the long, lonely struggle. He emerges from the conference with his adviser ready to learn from his supervisor. The fusion of school-agency breaks up. Immediately the student needs his supervisor, and he says good-by, in effect, to his adviser.

In the conference of adviser and supervisor following the student conference, the break-up of the fusion is complete. The adviser brings to the supervisor a brief account of the event that has occurred, an event that now is to become part of the student-supervisor relationship as it makes a new beginning.

Mr. W's supervisor wrote further in the mid-term evaluation: "After two weeks, I found an amazing difference in his work, a real sharing with and giving to his clients. This development has continued and he is truly 'reborn'. . . . With all this he is recognizing his own strength and has, for the first time, confidence in himself and in what he is doing. He is aware of change not only in the agency, but at home, with friends. . . ." This supervisor, like many another, may have felt that the amazing change took place quite apart from herself, off in that room where adviser and student met for an hour. What she came to know is what the school has long known: that without her weeks of seemingly unrewarding work with the student, without her having been the caring supervisor with high expectations for the student's performance in process, without her efforts to help the student learn, the adviser would have had nothing with which to concur. Without her expression of need and willingness to yield, there could have been no fusion. Without the supervisor, this amazing change could not have taken place. She could not have written: "He can now talk freely about this period and he sees that he was determined to work things out alone and was fighting desperately to keep me out of his learning experience. He refers now to that 'day two months ago. . . .' "

Another supervisor wrote in her mid-term evaluation, "It was not until after the adviser's visit that Miss A and I both discovered a new relationship in her learning. The result of this discovery has not always been easy. . . ." It is likely that no supervisor can live through this day's experience and find the student coming to him in need and wanting to learn, without feeling the changed relationship. It is likely, too, that though they begin anew, the long process of learning now opening will not be smooth. There will be other impacts and other choices, but the essential turning point has been passed with the student's act of positive willing.

Some educators and supervisors will say that not all students live the field experience with the necessity to meet such a crisis in their learning, that some students live life partially and learn gradually. Everyone lives life partially. This experience just described is itself a partial life experience; the individual living it makes it feel total to himself. The students who somehow get through the field work term missing the meeting with the single reality that they seek, keep seeking. They have been able through their camouflaged resistance and possibly their keen intelligence to defeat the school and the agency and in so doing have lost the battle themselves. The greater strength of the school-agency from which alone they might have truly learned, they never found; it was never offered to them.

Then there are the students who as in any school do not complete their work and withdraw, and there are those who are asked to withdraw. We have very few in either year, but we are not without them. As the growth-producing situation is not natural or catalytic or mechanical, but artificial and functional, it does not guarantee success every time. The student may refuse to take the step into learning when he has the opportunity, he may continue to defy the requirements of class and field, or he may simply not be equipped for study. He may find that life and growth for him lie in some other profession.

There also may be the rare occasion when the student cannot reach the important turning point because the school and agency have reached no relation of concurrence. In such a case, it may well be that the student's placement should be changed. In any exceptions to the process as it evolves for the great majority of students, thoughtful consideration of the concurrent school-agency relationship must be undertaken, and the particular process reviewed.

When concurrence has been achieved and the adviser has acted to take himself as the single fused reality to the student and has left to return to Chapel Hill, when the supervisor has discovered a new relation to the student who now is needing his help to learn and knows he needs it, all three are aware that the student has taken a giant step. Although far less sure of himself and of his knowledge and skill than he was when he arrived at the agency, he is aware of his growth in learning and his start toward becoming the helping person he hopes to be and believes his adviser and supervisor expect he can become.

6

CLASS WORK
AND FIELD WORK

One of the ways the Block Plan schools have devised to keep in touch with the student during the months of field work practice has been since the early days of the Smith College school to require written work of the student to be sent to the school at intervals. Block Plan schools have created a variety of written communications to and from the students while they are away from the campus in full-time field practice. Indeed, the use of such communications and assignments is part of the Block Plan almost without exception.

In the North Carolina school, the first-year students are given an assignment before they leave the campus for their field work. In this assignment, there are three topics for them to discuss, one due in Chapel Hill each month. The topics are related to the student's process of beginning in agency, of learning casework in practice, and of ending. The adviser reads the paper that the student writes and mails to him, and he responds as soon as possible though he may at the time be making field visits himself. These papers and the responses form the continuing connection of adviser and student in relationship and an important tie for the student with the school he has so recently come to know.

It is true that the casework teacher in this term has the function of field work adviser; but is that function any less than that of teacher? We have seen that, in his experience as adviser in the visit in which he acts to fuse school and agency, he does so through the teaching function at the heart of his chosen and designated work; and we could conjecture that although his students leave the campus, he does not desert this primary function. With each assignment he may have to reaffirm with himself that teaching and advising are part of the same element. So, in our examination of this structure of connecting students and adviser by mail over the miles, we see first that there is a teacher.

However, there is no classroom. The teacher, under the conditions of the Block Plan, cannot lecture or hold seminars or expect recitations while the student is in the field agency—three traditional means of teaching. Examinations, another of the primary methods of traditional pedagogy, can be taken by students individually. The written assignment is a close relative, pedagogically speaking, to the examination, and it can be met individually by each student wherever he is and apart from the sense of totality which so often accompanies the examination. By way of the assignment, we evolved a structure for the students to engage in school work while they were miles from the teacher and from each other.

When we mention "assignment," as we do in the North Carolina school and as other schools may or may not, we do not refer to an exchange of letters but to a student activity in some way related to the teaching function of the school. The teaching function of a school is usually considered as being fulfilled with a group of pupils in a class and through an immediate relationship of teacher and students. On the Block Plan, where there is no meeting on ·campus, the inference might then be that there can be no class and no teaching. As we considered the matter, on the other hand, it seemed to us that with our structure, wherein the adviser is also the casework teacher, assignments continued through the field work term might facilitate the learning of the student outside of a classroom.

After all, there is a class. The group of students who were together in the classroom during the campus term and had become acquainted with their classmates are now widely separated in their agencies located in five states and many cities and towns. They have no doubt, though, that a class with their own particular smaller section within it, composed of known and cherished individuals, now separated, will reconvene in the spring. Our hope is that the very writing of the papers contributes to the students' learning and doing of casework and gives them the opportunity to stop and think and feel, while they are removed from the busy life of the agency.

In the assignment papers, the adviser may sense beneath the content the student's attitude toward the agency. If the adviser considers it wise he might respond, as one first-year adviser did, to a student whose paper expressed indirectly his dismay over some unresolved and hitherto unmentioned difficulty in agency, in such a way that the student sought out the supervisor and brought him the difficulty directly. In a subsequent visit, the adviser and supervisor achieved concurrence in their relationship, and when the adviser took the further step to fusion of school-agency, the student who might have used his assignment as a means of continuing his connection with school as separate from agency found that the school-agency was really single. For the supervisor, who was new at this job, the student's writing to the school was at first somewhat threatening to him. In his experience with the adviser and the student arising from this initial exchange between student and adviser in the assignment, and the later visit of adviser to agency, the supervisor realized that he was not being overlooked and that in the adviser's eyes he was very much the man who did the teaching in the agency. In the beginning paper, in the in-between paper, or in the ending paper, the student may make use of his assignment in relating to agency and, in the course of writing, to the school.

For the second-year student, the assignment takes the same place in his learning process as it does for the first-year student, though there are differences. The first-year student writes more informally, as a rule, than does the second-year student, although he does not write a letter. The second-year student in writing more formally nevertheless writes of himself and his feeling as well as his thinking and doing. For both, the assignment itself and then the manner in which he replies allow the student to bring together once again in partial fashion his intellect-feeling, his theory-practice.

To present our interest in the nature of the assignment and its place in the concurrent process, we shall look closely at the second-year program with its longer time span and its greater number of assignments. A difference has come about in the course of developing each of the year's assignments for both years involved, and it has seemed right to us that this is so. No study has been made of the differences or of their relative effectiveness. Superficially, the chief differences in the second-year from the first-year assignments, aside from the formality, are the greater number of assignments, five for the five months; the greater complexity of the assignment questions; and the mailing of the assignments to the students each month while they are in the field. It has seemed to us to have had meaning to both first- and second-year students that the second-year assignments reflect the increasing knowledge and ability in helping of the more advanced students. Second-year students realize that they have left their first year behind them, and both classes respect the difference.

The timing of the assignments presented its practical as well as its pedagogical problems. For teachers who are traveling during the field work term and who have come to the firm conviction whether on campus or in the field that students' papers should have a response and be returned as quickly as possible, the timing was important. In both first- and second-year classes, the faculty decided that the interval of a month allowed them time to meet the various deadlines that were theirs.

With its longer field work time span and its advisory visits more widely spaced, the faculty for second-year students develop the assignments in process, and the composition of each assignment assumes immediate importance. The teacher has committed himself to teaching the group and not the individual; the assignment must be applicable to all students wherever they may be. The first question he may ask himself as he considers his group of students is where they all may be in relation to field work by the time the assignment reaches them. In approaching the composition of the first assignment, as an example, the teacher's question of himself is: where will the students be on September 15?

Physically, they will be scattered over five states, in very different social agency settings, different geographic locations, with different supervisors and executives, different services to render, and different clients. They are very different individual students, too. They all, however, will be trying to make themselves at home in their new surroundings, and meeting new experiences in the making.

The first assignment in second year usually includes a question about the student's beginning with a client and a summary of the interview. Another part of the assignment asks the student about his own impact in meeting with agency structure and how he is making it his own. Every student is able to answer these questions.

In response to the agency questions, one member of a recent class wrote:

I felt a certain sense of being unimportant. . . . I was shown my office which I was to share with another worker and there was only a chair standing in the space allotted to me. At this point I felt very resentful that the agency was not ready to accept me. I was given another worker's desk until her return from vacation. This did not feel too good to me. . . .

Now that I am settled in my own desk and chair, I can really appreciate the fact that it is mine . . . and the importance of physical structure.

and another:

This office was made my office before I ever saw it. . . . And I knew this at first glance because the agency had procured and placed on my desk a foot-long name plate with JANE C. BROWN in outstanding white letters. It was almost like a gift for me— name tag, keys and all.

and a third:

I had a choice of two desks and tried to decide in many ways— would the light be better here, the ventilation there, would it be colder in winter months here or there, would I be nearer the telephone? As the desk straddled a big water pipe, I could move it back and forth and this I did. Six inches back—the light was poorer, so I shifted again. . . . I was disappointed to learn that I would share the office with another student, and, then, later with still another one. . . . In addition, there is a drive that runs around the corner of the building and each vehicle that uses it, toots its horn directly over my desk.

I will, I am sure, become accustomed to these somewhat disturbing factors as time goes on. I am trying to make these things my own.

These students are writing of their own experiences, which are very much alive in the writing, and the negative in two of them is undisguised. In these papers they can express in safety their sense of disorganization and impact and the accompanying fear and resistance. But they are asked to do more. They are asked to tell what they are doing about it, what responsibility they are taking to make this new structure their own. The assignment is not simply an unburdening. It is also a part of the learning itself.

In the writing of his paper, the student may also realize that impact with structure is not a strange phenomenon. He had heard about it many times in class and yet had forgotten it again until it was he who met the impact. He may recall that his classmates are all writing about a similar event that they are experiencing wherever they are. He may realize, too, in working on the casework part of the assignment, that his client—whom he has just seen or will see tomorrow and who is new to him and the agency—may be living something of the same experience.

The student who writes, "I can really appreciate the fact that this is mine . . . and the importance of physical structure" has come through the experience of his negative reaction at impact, has taken to himself the necessity for some inner shift on his own part in order to begin to become a part of the agency, and has moved on to a learning of the universal underlying such an event. All of this he would probably say to his supervisor if the supervisor were there with him. But the universality of the importance of structure he brings to the university, and he sorts it out within the university where, indeed, it belongs.

When the papers are received, the teacher has first the duty of responding, but he also has the desire. These are communications from students with whom he has a relationship; their progress in the field and in the assignments are of concern to him. In the course of composing and responding to these assignments, our faculty came to a firmer grasp of what seemed to us to be our unique contribution to the student's learning. Student after student would introduce, as this student did, not only his relation to his own process and to his client's process, but also his relation to the underlying casework principles.

The very practice in agency is a major assignment offered by the school to the student; it is the professional half of his curriculum in becoming a social worker with a particular helping skill. The teacher-adviser cannot overlook the important content that is the student's day in and day out for these months and that he shares in part through the assignment; nor can the teacher-adviser rise above the tides of the student's relationship to school and to agency running beneath the content. When he comes to teaching, however, he needs to teach something different from that taught by the supervisor. He needs to recognize first the importance of the agency during the field work term and of the particulars that the student can learn only there. Yet he offers the student the opportunity and, more than that, the expectation to discover with his teacher at the university the universal ideas or concepts inextricably tied to practice, right at the university, which by its very nature represents these concepts.

The student who has moved past the first assignment has acted to move positively into learning when he met the single reality of his adviser's conference, and he has emerged newly to a true beginning with his supervisor. He is learning particular case by particular case. Vulnerable, full of feeling, mindful of his inadequacy and even of his hurtful attempts to make his clients over, he wants and needs the warm welcome and the help that his supervisor is extending to him and that his adviser confirmed was waiting for him. Who else but the supervisor can help him help the client who must have a serious operation and has no way to care

for her five small children? Who else but the supervisor
knows that this is not a "case," that this is Mrs. Brown and
that each of the children has a name and an individuality?
Who but the supervisor knows that the student wants so
much to help Mrs. Brown and yet is fearful of being unable
to? The supervisor is the one responsible for the help to the
client and to this particular client through the student. The
supervisor is the one who can help a person learn actually to
help.

Just as the campus teacher's process of teaching on
campus involves the student in experiential as well as intellectual learning, so the supervisor in the agency teaches
practice that involves the student in contentual as well as
experiential learning. The student can no more divide himself into two neat parts now that he is in field work than he
could while he was on campus. Yet the teacher cannot teach
practice and the supervisor cannot teach universal concepts,
or so we believe, as long as each is what he is.

In her second assignment and thus early in her experience at the agency, a student wrote that she hesitated to
begin to answer a question about her comprehension of and
relation to function, "for I do not really know the answers.
In class, I thought I understood function. When I first came
to the hospital I knew intellectually what my function
was . . . . I knew that my function was to help the patient to
leave the hospital . . . ." Then, after a paragraph of trying to
find her way, she writes, "I see as part of my function helping the patient look at his own feelings about leaving
here . . . if indeed he wants to leave. . . ." That he might
not want to leave had not been a part of her paper at the
start, and yet here it was. By the last paragraph, she was
saying, "But I have left something out and I do not know
how to say it. It is in regard to the use of myself as part of
this function. . . ."

The teacher to whom the student was writing did not

know Mr. Brown or Mr. Smith and did not know all the intricacies of discharge planning in this large psychiatric hospital. He did know about function and its relation to process; he did know about students and their relation to process. The student in her paper, which is very much a part of that process, is changing and growing as she writes and because she writes. As she struggles to find the words to convey her understanding to the university's teacher, the student feels her learning is particular and yet knows it is rooted in universal ideas that can make her experience communicable.

Later in the second-year field work term, another student, in writing of the concept and experience of yielding and of using help, said: "There is a great deal that remains for me to understand about this part of the process—post-turning point and ending. As I reflect upon this fact I realize that it may be due to my own current engagement in this part of my learning process and I, perhaps, have not yet incorporated full comprehension of this." Of course, she had not come to a full comprehension of this part of the helping process, nor for that matter of the beginning and turning point. No one is likely to, ever. For this student, in working first upon the theory and its exemplification in her own casework with clients, had come upon herself; and, if she had not, her teacher would have needed to point out her omission. The student searching in her fine, eager mind for a way through to comprehension found herself standing in her own way, herself engaged in the very process she was learning. The concepts of casework this student would master without difficulty. But to write of concepts to a university that, in its school of social work, could not separate concepts from experience, she was no longer so sure. She still had much to learn; consequently this discovery in the course of writing an assignment paper was of significance to her.

In the period that this student named the "post-turning point," learning in the agency is the first and important work of the student. His changed relationship to supervision is an awakening in himself from which arises the feeling for his clients which he has kept submerged. He can begin now to want to help and to care about helping his clients in their trouble. He no longer needs so heartily to prove himself. He begins to become identified with his helping function and is on his way to being the caseworker in his agency. Though he has far to go and much to learn, he belongs in the agency on which, as he now knows, both his learning for school and for agency depend. His adviser and supervisor share this knowledge with him.

We might ask whether, if it is so that the depth of his learning is and should be in agency, the attempt to keep a connection with the student, or teach him, does not tend to pull him away from the practice experience. It has seemed to us that no matter how far away from school a student gets in order to learn in agency, he remains fundamentally aware that being a social work student means being a student of the university. That this connection with school and university comes to the fore of his consciousness each time the assignment envelope is in his post box means that the relationship to the school which has been there all the time must now be newly acted upon. No supervisor has said that with the assignment the student left the agency psychologically; on the contrary, many say it has had meaning to students in the agency in varying degrees, even when it is evident that he had to work hard to complete it. Supervisor and adviser alike, however, keep aware of the possibility of the student's negative reaction to assignments in the unfolding of his process of learning and as part of the immediate relationship in agency or school.

For the teacher, working in process through assignments in this way, there can be a continuation of the active relationship of himself and class. The next month's assignment might take into account the responses of the previous month. For example, one month the papers of many of the individual students in the class indicated that they considered the assignment a very difficult one. And it was. Although they all tackled the assignment valiantly—one student using it as a means for reaching the supervisor as she had never before—they received the next month the teacher's recognition of the assignment's difficulty and of the students' wisdom and relatedness in so saying.

With two people teaching the student at the same time, whatever their respective content might be, two relationships are forming and moving under the content exchanged between teachers and student. There is a relationship between student and adviser as papers are written and responses are returned; there is a relationship of supervisor and student as the particular contents of agency, of clients, and of student are taken to and given a response by the supervisor. In both relationships, the presence of the other one may be resisted and denied, needed and used, but not eliminated. Between the points of concurrence and fusion run the human relationships of functionally connected individuals. In this "post-turning point" period, the school at times may seem peripheral to the student, who nevertheless recognizes its right and its necessity to speak to him individually and in the class, and to ask something of him.

When the teacher's response to the student assignment papers has been given consideration, it often has seemed to us as if possibilities are limitless. Should we be searching for a principle the teacher might employ as guide for his responses, we say that the obvious one would be to respond as a teacher commenting upon papers written by members of a casework class on campus. Such comments, spontaneously noted on the papers, give back the immediate feeling of the teacher to the student's having engaged himself wholly, with intellect, will, and feeling, and that if he has not done so, the expectation is held that he will. A pointing to another direction for his thinking or a gentle touch through the content to his feeling self provides new experiencing. Similar comments written on the student's papers from the field give us a guide and limit to response.

Spontaneous comments can be written on the student's papers, and yet we know so well that they cannot be received in immediacy. At a time when she was becoming more and more closely identified with her agency, a student wrote:

It seems that this assignment came at just the right time in relation to your question about staff. Up to this point I had been merely an observer, trying to learn some of the ways of working with patients as well as of presenting what the worker had done in the relationship. Yesterday, Tuesday, November 25, my feelings and status changed. I had to present two cases to staff.... I am really becoming a part of the program and playing a vital role in helping patients.... I no longer feel I am an "outsider" or observer, but a part....

This would seem to be a triumph shared in the belief that she would be understood and that her rejoicing would be her adviser's, too—a paean of delight in growth and learning which could be acknowledged in kind. How she really had, in fact, presented her cases in staff, her supervisor knew and would tell the adviser in due time. We might doubt that the first time was as full of delight for the staff as for the student; we cannot be sure. The adviser is in no position to express doubt. He does not know the case; he does not see the student present it. He is related to the student, and he need not hesitate to respond so that she can feel his enjoying the moment with her.

As soon as we say "enjoy the moment," we have to ask in all honesty, what moment? There are no moments to enjoy; there is no immediacy. Five days elapsed between this student's dropping her paper in the mailbox and receiving her adviser's reply. By that time, surely her excitement had dimmed. Except for two days in the field work term, there is no immediacy in the adviser-student relationship.

Yet, somehow, that does not ring true, either. Even now, reading the student's words "Tuesday, November 25," there is an immediacy of a memorable day. The teacher's response, spontaneously noted on the paper and returned as quickly as possible, is received by the student who, although he may by this time be in a slough of despondency over an error made in his practice, can catch the quality of response from a safe person and place in Chapel Hill. There is no actual immediacy. But the adviser's response written spontaneously, not aimed to change the student's activities directly as in supervision but nudging him in the direction of increasing his understanding and responsibility for it, may feel spontaneous when received. The response may be little different from the kind a teacher might make on student papers during the campus term.

Questions that are directed outside the casework relationship we try to time for that place in their process when students are having or have had experiences with staff as well as professional and lay members of the community. Of course, the timing is often uneven. For most of the students, however, their experience moves outward until at the close of the term each has had some experience in working with the community in the natural course of his caseload's exigencies. The assignment asks for the student's awareness of change in his responsibility for his own part as an agency caseworker in meeting real and not hypothetical administrative, group, or community organization situations. As the student who wrote the above paper showed so clearly, the timing was exactly right for her. She was learning about staff relations practically; and, in writing about their importance and her responsibility, she was en route to an understanding at her own level.

Earlier we mentioned that an adviser in response might assist the student when the evidence is in the paper, and the adviser is attuned sensitively to it, to seek and find his supervisor. In so doing, the adviser is actually clarifying for himself and for the student how much of the student's learning problems he takes at this time to the supervisor and agency and how much to school. He is drawing the limits to the adviser's job and thus also to the supervisor's. Such functional differentiation has in it a dynamic for relationship as each of the two—adviser and supervisor—grows to accept his own limits and that of the other. This same differentiating is a dynamic for the student as he relates to each of these whose clarity, rather than willing fuzziness, he needs. It seems too obvious to mention that the face-to-face relationship during the field work term is not the adviser's. The student's actual performance in staff, his ire at the doctor, his helpfulness on the case, his relationship to supervision, can be judged by the supervisor who is there to see. Although the adviser needs to be attuned to the student's projections upon him which should be directed to agency, he also realizes that he must not arouse in his response matters that he could ordinarily take up with the student in a conference were the student on campus.

The student who sends in a very thoroughly prepared paper but who has answered one of the questions from an incorrect reading poses a problem. Why did he misread the question? Is he resisting the school or the agency? What should the adviser do in response? With one student who made this mistake, the adviser replied first with recognition of his work in the rest of his paper and of a recent visit made to the agency, and then pointed out the error, asking that the student do that section of the assignment over and return it to the adviser in a week. Responsibly and without apology, the student had his rewritten question at the school from his placement four hundred miles away within the stated time. This learning of responsibility was an experience for the student which a response directed to possible cause might have prevented his having.

Not only in the response but also in the composition of the assignment itself, we try to take into consideration the fact of the adviser's visit to the agency. The first assignment, for example, has been written and returned by the time of the first visit. The second assignment has been received by most students by the time of the second visit. The third assignment is composed and mailed after all of the first visits have been made to the agency and all of the students have seen their advisers. The assignments themselves can carry the adviser's awareness of this movement of the process for all members of the class.

In this "post-turning point" period, as we have mentioned, the student often shows an immediate improvement in his work as he begins anew to learn. He is beginning to help clients for whom he has until now been inaccessible. He does, however, have to continue to be helpful, and, as time goes on, he is not able to be helpful in the way his supervisor expects him to be or as he expects himself to be.

Toward the end of November, the mid-term evaluation conference takes place, and the supervisor's written report is due in the agency around December 1. (This is the evaluation report from which we quoted in the preceding chapter.) Our experience has led us to believe that this conference, held in a regular supervisory conference period, marks an ending to the first half of the field work experience. The evaluation conference is a time of pausing, of reflection, of standing aside and looking at the actual performance in learning and in helping—by both student and supervisor. It is, in fact, a time of carefully and authoritatively carried out evaluation by the supervisor, who must share his criticisms, positive and negative, with school as well as with student. But the sense of ending marked by this conference carries with it also the sense of a new beginning. This time the student's process begins to move toward its actual ending of the field work term in February. Once again the student pushes against his supervisor and becomes enmeshed in his will to prove himself. The necessity for a second turning point arises, this time with the supervisor who until January will not have the adviser with him to be the single reality the student is once more pushing toward. The supervisor now becomes the person he really is—a professional staff member of a particular agency charged with helping clients and for the time being with helping them through the teaching of the student.

One supervisor wrote in her final evaluation in February that Mr. Y continued

to test the supervisor until the middle of December when we had a very stormy conference session. This climaxed his attempts to control learning from me by contending it was in opposition to theory learned at the school. I was aroused to the point where I had to remind him that he was working for the agency and in that setting I was responsible for what happened to clients, not the school. . . .

Although this was an extremely difficult experience for both of us, it proved to be the real turning point for Mr. Y. Since then I have felt a shift from testing me as a supervisor to using me as a way to test his own knowledge and skill. He seems much less tense and anxious . . . he has made tremendous strides in demonstrating casework ability. . . .

The supervisor was truly the supervisor with this strong student. She had no time to inquire whether the school content and agency practice were or were not alike on this matter, and she could not assume that they were, even with the achievement of school-agency concurrence in October.

She acted as the person she was. Standing squarely upon her function in an agency for helping clients, she elected to take the one way in which Mr. Y could discover in her the strong supervisor he was demanding. Had she debated, hesitated, wondered how she could relieve this student of the stress he was obviously undergoing, had she tried to be "understanding," she would have been lost and so would he.

During the same month, December, Mr. Y had written a paper in answer to the assignment question that the faculty formulated to give the student an opportunity to work, internally and then on paper, on his understanding for himself and for his clients of the yielding experience. Mr. Y's reply, in part follows:

The client's denial of the need for help, whether the denial is masked or proclaimed, is a device for shutting out the other person.... When the client discovers the helping person as a resource that is working with, rather than against him, he finds an altogether different climate in which to work. Actually, the climate is the same but his perception of it has changed. He finds the helping person as an ally that is steady and dependable—one who is willing to leave the eventual direction of change in the hands of the client while at the same time holding to what is real and fixed of the reality that prevails. This is the turning point; the moment of choice; the beginning of the end.... It is the discovery that opens the way for the client as well as the student to trust enough, to "risk," and to make far more use of the available help than previously had been the case.

Mr. Y is speaking of himself. Although he has not the skill to be the helping person he describes, he may, as students often do, review the case record of a client who has made a simple shift to taking responsibility for some action, and find in it all the elements of the turning point he mentions. It is true that they are all there, in microcosm. Still, it is primarily of himself that he speaks. His experience in October with the adviser as the single reality he chose for the fulfillment of his life in learning, and his experience in December with his supervisor as the reality of agency supported, as he knew, by the school, he could also express. The content of his paper out of context might read as if it were objectively written; he and the reader, who was the adviser, knew that it was full of feeling. By February, the adviser's evaluation of Mr. Y's class work in the field concurred with his supervisor's summation in the final evaluation: "Mr. Y's progress during these last two months of his field work has been quite remarkable."

For all students, by the second and final advisory conference, some similar experience occurs, although not always with the intensity of Mr. Y's nor in the same manner. The students by this time have been writing papers for their school assignments with considerable depth of thought and feeling in an effort to bring form to their learning as well as expression of their own learning process. They have not been able to bridge the gap that reopens between school and agency, practice and theory, as they feel it in the split structure. Their projections of the best of themselves into their papers and practice cannot be sustained as the time for the adviser's visit nears. They need to have the school-agency with them again in reality before they move to the conclusion of field work.

With another student the second turning point came about differently from Mr. Y's. The supervisor wrote that by mid-term, Mrs. Z had met the main expectations of second year and was fully involved in learning. Then, in the final evaluation, she observed: "After Christmas, Mrs. Z became angry with me because I was not pushing her to learn more—insulted by my willingness to let her be—and told me so with some sting. She said that I could stay that way if I wanted to but she was not willing to accept that she was as good as she could be—she was going to do something about it!" After Christmas the students of the second-year class begin to sense that the ending of field work is coming into sight. In January their adviser will make a second and last visit; in February they will return to campus. Mrs. Z may well have been feeling some of the weight of ending in her need to make the fullest use of the remaining time and of the supervisor. The negative in "You haven't given me enough!" so often felt in ending can be a powerful dynamic for redoubled learning. On the other hand, students can also be caught in this negative if adviser and supervisor do not act. Mrs. Z did, in fact, have much yet to learn.

When her adviser visited in January, Mrs. Z pressed for verification that she was not going to be accepted for less than she could be. Her conference with her adviser followed, as it had in October, a conference between her adviser and supervisor in which once again they had reached the point of concurrence. Once again, the adviser represented the single reality of school and agency which alone would satisfy Mrs. Z. She discovered that, through her adviser, the school-agency expected her to be the helping person she could be and not simply to rejoice in the anticipation of her own potential. For her, this new fusion of school-agency could make possible her single act of choosing again to learn as she approached the term's ending. Such fusion may well feel to a student like Steiner's "integration," which he saw when supervisor and adviser were actually the same person!

In the structure of our second year, the adviser's second visit comes within four to six weeks of the student's leaving the field agency to return to the campus. In this last visit of the adviser, we have adopted the practice of giving the student official university recognition of his having earned field work credit, if he has, and provided of course that his work continues its prevailing quality. It has seemed to us that only the adviser, representing the school and the university, should confirm with the student what he wants so much to hear—that he has passed the course. He hears it before he leaves the field work agency.

For most students this confirmation of a job well done comes as no surprise and yet until the responsible authority says so, there is always a shred of doubt. For some students, this word from the adviser comes as a relief and an impetus for productive learning in the last few weeks. With supervisor in conference and adviser in papers, the student has not been unaware of his progress all along; with the adviser on this day, he receives the significant and authoritative word.

In saying that the student receives this word from his adviser, we mean he receives the word from his adviser as the fused school-agency. In their conference together, adviser and supervisor discuss and come to an agreement about the student's work for the year; they affirm their feeling of having been working together contemporaneously through these months; once again they yield and take responsibility. The supervisor is approaching the ending of his functional process of teaching the student to help the clients of the agency. Momentarily he lets go of his teaching function, which once again the adviser assumes. The adviser, at this same time, is approaching the ending of the school-agency process with which he must identify in order to contain within himself the fused school-agency. He is also approaching the start of the final term's process with the student who will be returning to his class on campus.

In this final conference for second-year students, there arises also the matter of introducing the student to a preliminary exploration of his area of interest for the final major professional study or essay that he will write in the spring term. Sometimes we have thought it to be too soon to catapult the student into matters pertaining so particularly to school while he is still in the field; and yet we know that we are not doing the catapulting—the student himself is. He would have the greatest difficulty in refraining from asking, "But what shall I do about the essay?" should the adviser try to keep the subject hidden. It cannot be hidden. It is foremost in the student's thoughts and feelings each time he glances toward the campus during mid-winter. So it is that the subject is introduced and briefly discussed.

When the student has come to this near-ending part of his learning process in the field, and has had the recognition of adviser and supervisor that his work has been satisfactory, he can enter into productive weeks in agency. A sense of relief and accomplishment is with him, and the assurance of being needed by the agency as one of its caseworkers is gratifying. The need to learn and to make use of the remaining days of his student life in practice has been renewed. Before the student leaves, he will have an evaluation conference with his supervisor. The focus of the conference is the student and the work he has done, the work he is doing, and the work he may look forward to doing when he once again is helping clients of a social agency. This evaluation is part of the student's ending with agency.

His supervisor may feel—and we hope this is so for each supervisor—a reward for the work he has done in helping this student become a caseworker.

The final assignment looks in two directions. Its questions pertain to endings: the ending of the student with agency and the ending of student with client. Its questions have also to do with beginnings, that is, with the preparation for beginning. The student is asked to send case material to the school for use in class during the spring term, and he is asked to specify his topic for his professional essay. The second-year student leaves the agency in mid-February and returns to the campus for the final term.

Three weeks later, the first-year students who have also been in agency during the winter will be in the midst of their preparations for leaving and beginning. They will be writing their final assignment and selecting the case material that they will present to class in the spring term. They may share the feeling of this student, who wrote in his final assignment, "During my work in this field placement, it has been a rewarding experience to see my patients move from the beginning of the process to the end.... Now that I am beginning to end with them and help them end with me, and go on to their next worker, I find I have a deeper feeling for them.... I think one reason for my feeling as I do about this ending is because I, too, am ending a process—a process in which I have moved from beginning to, now, the ending with my supervisor...." For him, at least, the months of field work were, as he wrote, time enough in which to learn and to bring about a positive creative ending. It would not be surprising if at some place during this ending, he had not discovered along with Mrs. Z and many of his classmates, that he needed more—more from himself, his supervisor, and time! He and the other students of the school have, as a matter of fact, helped clients; and this above all is their achievement in first and in second year of field practice, each student according to his own ability. Now they journey toward school. In the space of one long weekend, they undergo the amazing metamorphosis from dignified agency caseworkers to campus students.

7

ACHIEVING A COMMENCEMENT

The life of the university is in full tide as the spring term of the University of North Carolina School of Social Work begins. Nine thousand students, graduate and undergraduate, have been attending classes and games and lectures and concerts since September, and into their midst now come the social work students. The student social worker can hardly escape feeling different from the other students of the university or escape a feeling of likeness and reunion with the fellow classmates he greets. The importance of the university and of the student's peers as part of his learning which transcends the classroom is evident as the student again takes his place in campus life.

Although the spring term is like the first campus term for the North Carolina social work students in having class work without field work, it is different from that term in a number of ways. In the first place, the past of agency and practice is a past shared with the adviser. This common past cannot be eradicated by them; it cannot be unlived. It may be, as a matter of fact, a link between the school and the student in relation to agency. In the second place, the student brings with him the irreversible change within him.

He has grown; he is not the same person he was those months before. And, thirdly, he has achieved a degree of competence in helping which he did not possess in his first campus term and which he prizes and cannot practice again until after the school year's end.

The mention of the swift change of locale, the swift metamorphosis from agency caseworker to campus student, which we see taking place with each student year after year, by no means implies that his internal change from agency to campus is completed so swiftly. The informal dress so delightedly worn on the first day back is a symbol of change in the making and not of the change having been made. Beneath the competent, if casual, exterior is the tightly willed organization of the returning student beginning his final term with a high and ongoing belief in his accomplishment in practice, in his knowledge, his growth, and his understanding. Once again he says the words of wanting to learn and grips a book that somehow seems to take the place of his temporarily lost helping function. And once again he undertakes the human process of movement into a new relationship with previously known adviser and professors. We see the task of the school in large part as making it possible for the student to release his inner life again and to find in the campus term a new learning and a new creativity with which he can leave school in June, fulfilled and fulfilling. The task, as we see it, now more than ever before, entails offering him learning which is both contentual and experiential as one who is being helped to learn and who has been a helper himself.

Although there is no structure for the concurrent relationship to continue after good-bys have been said to the supervisor and agency by the first-year student and adviser, the agency still has its place in the spring term. The first-year student begins in casework class and presents his own case material to the class. As he experiences for the first time the sharing of his own work in the classroom, his fellow classmates experience for the first time the reception of the recorded cases presented by their contemporaries. For the student presenting the case, the hour is a learning one, not just in the content exchanged and suggestions made but also in finding himself more fully engaged in the present process far from the agency. For the students who are in the position of critic, safe at the moment from any revelations of their own, there is learning of casework problems and principles for their solution in settings new to them and also in the use of themselves as constructive critics.

The fact that student cases are not skillfully handled has often raised doubt in the minds of educators who do not employ this method in their teaching. We believe that the values of learning through being the leader or being a member of the audience in discussing even the simplest first-year case exceed those of continued discussion of cases that have no live connection with the students. The teacher, of course, is always the teacher and along the way will introduce case material from outside the students' own field practice at intervals when the intensive examination of their own work needs to be broken up. He will also give assignments for reading and for the students' written work, both of which may form a nucleus of the next class discussion.

The casework teacher-adviser whether first or second year, now that he has his students once more in the classroom, may be tempted to act in a quasi-supervisory capacity when the student's case is being presented. His identification with his teaching function, which is that he teach all the students, prevents him from so doing as does his realization that the student cannot take the particular suggestion into practice. He is there for the students' learning of basic principles underlying casework as they have been actualized in their own past practice. It never fails to be astonishing that students are able to relate their field work experience to the class work with a freshness that even after two months on campus, as it must be for some students, still seems almost current.

This freshness, as we have seen it and felt it in many classes, has seemed to us possible of release by the student partly through the teacher's having achieved a concurrence with the student's supervisor during the practice term and the student's awareness of this concurrence. He does not bring to his classmates the evidence of his own practice born out of school-agency strife and sharp difference. He can speak with confidence about a school-approved agency, a firm agency-school relationship, and his own practice, which, if far from perfect, was acceptable to both supervisor and teacher. In this fresh re-living of an important life experience in helping a client, there is also the heightened expectation that the student feels for himself and from his teacher to present himself well as caseworker in his agency. He sometimes forgets, but he soon discovers again in class that he is also there to learn. The remarkable moments he spent with his client, if not remembered accurately or chronologically, for such is the way of memory, are imbued with the liveliness of the present relationships with teacher and with fellow classmates.

Of course, in this lively present, the negative as well as the positive feelings may appear in the class presentation as well as toward the student's practice, or the student may project his present fears upon the absent agency. The teacher in the classroom relationship may need to act as school-agency and take upon himself what is indeed present though it may be designated by the student as past. The teacher cannot call in the agency for verification; he must represent the agency insofar as concurrence has been achieved by school and agency. Where the teacher finds an honest difference with agency in the case as it unfolds in class, he has the duty to his students to express it and can do so aware that he would also make known this same difference to the supervisor were he present. Difference does exist in the closest of relationships, and its expression need not destroy the relationship.

Once again, the course in "Psychological Backgrounds for the Helping Professions" accompanies the casework course in first year as the core of the practice curriculum. The spring term of this course has quite a different content from that of the fall term, and with the first class the student begins a renewed relationship with the same teacher of the fall. As the students return from being so far away physically and psychologically from school and from a course such as this one, it is not surprising that they feel its impact again. Engaged as they had become with their supervisors and advisers and clients in new depths of learning in relationship, they begin as in all beginnings, tight with will and determined this time to meet no obstacles to their further learning. Once again, they come to learn that the obstacle to their learning is within themselves.

The content of the psychological backgrounds course in the spring term, as in the fall term, may be categorized under the heading usually made by social work educators as "Human Growth and Development." The teaching of the course recognizes, as in the fall, that psychological content is closely tied by the student to his own growth and development. An understanding of such psychological problems as the relation of fate and self-responsibility, need and satisfaction of need, union and separation, self and "other" comes about, we believe, when the student can make them real for himself. This he can do in the process of relating past to present while reading and writing papers about the growth of the self from conception through later life. The difference in this course, again as in the fall term, lies in the fact that the human being who grows and develops during the spring term is not simply the other fellow, but the social work student himself. For some students, not all to the same extent, an understanding that is immediate sustains their actual change from fearful blame, usually on parents, to an assumption of responsibility for their own part in incidents in the past which hitherto they had considered traumatically damaging.

Along with these two courses, "Casework" and "Psychological Backgrounds," which are closely related in process though not actually in content, the other courses in group process, research, child and public welfare, and medical information continue with the same professors who taught the courses in the fall. As the weeks go by and as the ending of the term comes into view, the students realize that it cannot be completed without a decision's being made about their returning in the summer for a second year.

The process of moving to second year is carried by the adviser with the student. In mid-April, the first-year advisers make known to the students the faculty's recommendation whether the student will be allowed to continue into second year or not. There is the occasional student for whom it is suggested that he work for a year or so and then come back for his second year, or the student for whom it is suggested that another professional field would be advisable. The adviser has the responsibility for helping these students to a positive ending. For the student who is recommended to second year and who in the first conference with the adviser indicates a desire to continue, there are several other steps to be taken in the process.

The adviser, in his second conference with the student, tells him of the second-year field work placement that is his and that as nearly as possible meets the student's interest in the type of agency, his needs to be near Chapel Hill if married and responsible for a family there, and his request for available financial assistance. In the course of coming to a firm "yes" to a second year and to this particular placement, students sometimes live through considerable turmoil, indecision, fear, and resistance—in fact, they often experience their major turning point of the term in respect to this field placement content. Others find that the placement meets exactly their own projections of what they wanted, and the process of choosing seems for the most part a relief and joy. It is impossible to know ahead of time what the student's reaction will be or how responsibly he will consider what is offered to him. We do know that a great deal of thought in evaluation of students and placements goes into the field work assignment and its place in the student's process in school.

After the student has come to affirm the placement for himself and the school, he has yet another step to take before the suggested agency is his. He makes a visit to the agency to meet with the executive and, on some occasions, with his new supervisor. Presenting himself almost as though in job application, he receives from the executive the positive word of the agency's agreement to his placement and stipend, if there is to be one, and returns once more to his adviser to bring word of the trip. The student has made his choice, and the placement to which he will go in September is his.

At the close of his first-year casework class, the student writes a final term paper on a topic of his own choosing. This is a major piece of writing concerned with casework and with his own relating of theory to practice in casework. The term paper is the culmination of a long, busy year and through it, we hope, he can express himself as he feels himself to be—whole and integrated, having learned and changed, and grown, moving yet toward fulfillment of his inner potential. By means of this paper, we have tried to give him an opportunity to reach at the termination of first year a veritable commencement, an ending and a beginning. From his point of view and from that of his teachers who have for so long been engaged with him in this process, he has indeed earned it. The supervisor may not be present for this commencement, which is after all necessarily spelled with a lower case *c,* but there is no question that he has been there. And there is no question that his agency has been right there along with him, through the term and into the final paper by means of the student's own experience in agency and of adviser-supervisor concurrence.

In the spring term of the second-year casework sequence at the University of North Carolina School of Social Work, the student takes one elective course and a course in psychopathology. In addition, two courses provide for the inclusion of agency-learned skill in the final term: a seminar in "Social Casework"; and a course, "Studies in Social Work Process," taught by the tutorial method. These four courses continue throughout the fourteen-week term. As we have already noted, preliminary action for casework class and for the writing project is taken by the student while he is still in agency. The case material for these courses precedes him to the campus, and the teacher has the opportunity to read the cases before the student arrives. By the time the student comes for his first campus conference with his adviser-teacher, he finds that his case material and his selection of an essay topic have been read and are to be part of the content of that conference.

The student presents one of these cases in the casework class as he did in his first year; but that was a year ago. The impact of facing his fellow-students with his own record and of taking responsibility for the discussion to a greater extent than he had in his first year is still unavoidable if he cares about himself, his agency, and his learning. Whatever is said in the classroom, he can do nothing about in practice. He cannot remedy an error; he cannot seek the solace of a supervisor; he cannot take fresh theory to agency next week.

His learning must be right here in the classroom at the moment.

Through his work in class, the student learns of process, not skill. He cannot learn a skill in helping while sitting at a seminar table. However, as he reaches his positive relation to learning in this course and quickens his understanding, he seems to become convinced that he has been sharpening his helping skill. The faculty has sometimes considered this sense of increasing skill to have become so real to the students that they have warned that this cannot be and not to expect it when they are in agency again. Although it is probably wise for us to give such a warning, it actually means little. As he rejoices in his own campus learning and becomes confident of his growing skill, it is likely that what is real in relation to skill is that through the campus learning in content and experience, he has become conscious of his increasing ability to gain skill when he is in practice. The immediacy of understanding and relationship in the casework class and the psychological backgrounds class, and in the other classes, too, has contributed to the feeling that the present experiencing is of his whole self, the practical as well as the theoretical.

The traditional structure long relied upon in universities for the completion of a period of graduate study has been the thesis. Either as analytic reasoning or as empirical research, the thesis seemed to the faculty of our school as unsuited for the student who wanted to write of his own growth and practice. On the other hand, we realized that for him to write in complete reliance upon personal feelings presented the hazard of a lack of disciplined thought. As the faculty of the University of North Carolina School of Social Work reviewed theses year after year, it became apparent to us that the student needed to be released from the dual expectation placed upon him to include research requirements and the personal attainment of casework knowledge and skill in the same thesis. We acted to place the research project for each student, either individually or as part of a group, in the first-year curriculum and to place the individual writing requirement in the second-year curriculum.

The question that the casework faculty then asked themselves was whether any traditional form existed which would allow for the inclusion of feeling as well as thinking, for practice as well as theory, and which would also provide orderly limits. We found such a form. The students were asked to write an essay.

The essay is a legitimate literary form. It carries the sanction of time and tradition to writing which has in the past contributed to the advancement of knowledge, good writing, and human feeling—and is at present coming into its own again in much current literary and professional writing. For professional social work writing, we at first hesitated; the essay seemed to connote a familiarity and looseness of writing which modern social work would surely not condone. When we looked further, however, we discovered that writing such as Schrecker's *Work and History*[1] was subtitled *An Essay on Civilization* and that one of Cassirer's major works was titled *An Essay on Man.*[2] Anyone who has read either book will certainly agree that neither is a familiar essay like those written by Emerson. And anyone who has read Emerson's essays knows that they include much besides familiar anecdotes. This and other outside evidence met what we were approaching from within. We became less fearful of the word *essay* and more convinced that the meanings of the words in the term *professional essay* were not contradictory. Since it seemed quite possible to write an essay and still be professional, we

1. Paul Schrecker, *Work and History: An Essay on Civilization* (Princeton: Princeton University Press, 1948).
2. Ernst Cassirer, *An Essay on Man* (New Haven: Yale University Press, 1944).

decided that the essay might hold just what we sought for our student writing project.

There was one element missing. The essay did not have, as far as we knew, any internal form or structure to serve as a guide for the student. We were wrong. The essay has a sturdy form that we could present to students. This basic form as outlined by Read[3] is:

1. A beginning on familiar ground
2. Announcement of a paradoxical theme, which is to be the subject of the essay
3. Development of the theme by appeal to common experience, etc.
4. Illustration of the theme by anecdote
5. Deduction from the illustration
6. Summary of theme and statement of moral

The form as actually worked out with the student becomes:

1. A beginning on familiar ground and location of the self in the learning process.
2. Announcement of a paradoxical theme, focus of interest, cliché, or misunderstood phrase that is to be the subject of the essay.
3. Development of the theme by appeal to experience:
   a. common human experience
   b. own learning experience
   c. professional experience of others
   d. recognition of own relation to the past
4. Illustration of theme by case record from own professional helping in second-year field work agency.
5. Discussion of the case and the helping process as related to topic.
6. Summary of theme and statement of meaning to self and others.

3. Herbert Read, *English Prose Style* (Boston: The Beacon Press, 1955), p. 71.

Within this form, within the boundaries of the essay, the students might bring order to their thinking and feeling and introduce a case of their own, recorded and discussed in process as illustration of their understanding and practice. The students would not need to depend upon some *a priori* statement from which to deduce their remarks in the essay; they had the generative principle out of which they could write as they had learned. In what had been created in their heritage, and with what spirit, they had a guide for uncovering the new for themselves in their essays and perhaps for furthering a desire to uncover the new for others some day. With this form at hand, we put into practice the essay as the final major writing assignment of the two years of study in social casework.

The students have been eager to tackle the themes they selected for their essays—and the themes they select are not small ones. Some of the topics would take a dissertation to explore and some a lifetime; but students are not expected to plumb the depths of their subjects. Topics like these have been chosen by students and reflect the initial instructions for preparing the essay: a focus of interest, a cliché, a paradox:

That there can be a richer union with one who can claim and affirm his own difference seems paradoxical. Is not difference a separating rather than a uniting factor in relationship?

and:

Can casework be offered effectively in a court setting where an outstanding characteristic of the court is authority?

and:

My main purpose in writing this paper is to explore and to discuss the idea—Help Can Be Used By Those Who Did Not Seek It. It is basically my personal interest and hope to try to clarify this concept for myself in retrospect to my learning experience in a protective service.... To a large extent, my main interest in this paper stems from the earth of practical experience.

and :

I have wondered why, if a person appeals to me for help, he resists it at the same time. This, I must admit has bothered me and really kept me thinking and seeking an answer.

As the students begin their writing of the essays with bi-weekly tutorial conferences, the essay places limits upon the student's human desire to work in his own way. What might seem the somewhat loose requirements imposed by the essay's form nevertheless does provide the important content of a process in which they become engaged newly with the adviser. At times, as had been true for the thesis, the writing of the essay has seemed to comprise for the student the whole of his school experience. The shift that the students make in the course of writing the essay often becomes the major turning point of this final term.

There was the student whose hard-won academic training caused her to object to the informality of the essay and to the requirement that she not write her observations as though she existed apart from the human scene. The vigor of her resistance extended to the agency and the school because also of what she considered and for what had been, in fact, a difficult field work term. Her resistance was so great that she seemed unlikely to finish her essay; she denied her learning and the beginning skill that she had been helped to gain in school and agency. It might seem that the road to professional salvation for such a student, a very able student, would lie through the adviser's finding some way to produce a concurrence of school-agency in order that she might come upon the limits and the giving of both school and agency and cease her flailing at one or the other. In

actuality, in this term there is no way to draw the agency
back into the school, even if this plan were a practicable one.
An alternative gave the student the incentive she needed.
She was held by her adviser to the required form and to
work according to the specifications or to cease doing it at
all. She chose to learn and to grow. She met the requirements and completed her essay, surprised to find out for
herself that intellect and feeling together made her essay
writing creative.

Another student, whose placement experience had been
fully a learning one, began to write her essay with considerable outward confidence and organization. After about three
weeks, she became bogged down in her words, and, in panic,
came to her adviser saying that she had to return to the
agency three hundred miles away to get another case to
substitute for the one she had selected, one that she now
deemed entirely inadequate. Here again it might seem that
the agency could be drawn into the process, and perhaps a
kind of concurrence could be produced which would help
the student find what she needed for her writing. Instead,
the adviser refused the student's request; the directions for
securing case material before returning to school had been
specific. At this place in her process, the student needed
neither case nor supervisor. She needed to have the limit
placed upon her which she could use, as she did, to stop and
look at herself fleeing outward for her solution. On the next
day she was for the first time in that term psychologically
located at the school, relieved and ready to write her essay.

A third student brought to his writing such an over-
flowing feeling of his own growth and change and gratitude
for his field work opportunity that he wanted to write a
personal testimonial as an essay. Recognizing the joy he was
expressing, the adviser asked him to follow the essay's form
and to acknowledge his relation to the world of knowledge
and experience outside of himself as well as inside. Meeting

these requirements came as a sharp impact to this student, and he responded with an angry withdrawal followed by a shift to a positive relatedness to school and to adviser which enhanced his tribute to his agency as well as his achievement in learning.

The completed essays, properly typed and bound, are available for reading by all students. Sometimes, they have served as an impetus for the development of further work on similar topics. For example, one student in closing her essay on the nature of caring in casework said: "I feel that to care deeply is to live fully. To face life courageously, as it unfolds with all its joys and suffering, strengthens the feeling of the self, alone, while deepening the self's awareness of the need for others in his continual striving toward fuller growth. This, to me, is the underlying meaning of caring in a casework relationship."[4] A student in the succeeding year elected to write on "caring" too and carried forward this student's contribution to a further comprehension of a casework process in which the caring of the caseworker became part of the very difficult job of sustaining the helping function in process with a man who was aphasic.[5]

Another student, in writing about choice in the adoption application, said:

It seemed to me that Mrs. Lewis was beginning to see that the real choice she must make was not whether or not to adopt a baby, but whether she would use help in finding out if adoption was the answer to her need. This was the initial choice and the one which could come only from within. This initial choice is the choice of life and growth regardless of the numbers of

4. Dolly Sanders Thompson, "Discovering the Meaning of Caring in a Casework Relationship," unpublished essay (Studies in Social Work Process, University of North Carolina, School of Social Work, 1961), p. 29.

5. Sara Adams Oliver, "Finding a Freedom to Care: Its Importance in Helping Psychiatric Patients Accept Hospitalization," unpublished essay (Studies in Social Work Process, University of North Carolina, School of Social Work, 1962).

possible reality choices which had seemed to cloud the air or
the lack of them which appeared to offer only submission and
bitterness as a reward. This is the choice which gives the self
freedom, which enables the self to become responsible for its
further choices in determining its ultimate destiny. This is
the choice I offered Mrs. Lewis at our next interview.[6]

Although many of these words may have been expressed
and written before, this student is creating in her essay her
own understanding of a concept and experience that she has
known for herself and has been able to use in practice. The
deceptively simple nature of the essay might hide the fact
that the student in work important in its creativity for
herself also discusses an aspect of choice not always seen by
students. We have considered that, with more advanced students, the essay may well have in it the necessary ingredients
for seeing and saying what formal research and analytic
exposition cannot.

It may be that the student's will, in carrying out the
individual impulse or urge for functional creativity, brings
about within the one person a union of the separate elements,
academic and professional, and creates the "philosopher-
practitioner" whom long ago Elizabeth Macadam coveted for
the social worker. This union within the social worker
would also have eased the fears of Frances Morse sixty-five
years ago when she foresaw the educated social workers
(we, her descendants with master's and doctor's degrees)
thinking that we would know more than we do. In the integrating within themselves of will-impulse-feeling-intellect,
the writing of the essay becomes truly the student's own creation. Each student out of his newly won integration as he
completes his two years of study and practice expresses this
wholeness in his writing, a wholeness that he recognizes

6. Mary Elizabeth English, "Choice in the Application to Adopt a
Child," unpublished essay (Studies in Social Work Process, University
of North Carolina, School of Social Work, 1961), pp. 19-20.

would not be his without present helpers and past pioneers. As one student wrote, "And so it has turned out that with my desire to learn to help, and with the school and agency providing me with an experience in which I was helped to find my own useful strengths, I have moved to the point of being able to offer help to some limited degree. . . . The emotional experience combined with the intellectual learning has made the process of learning fully a living experience."

The feeling that this student has of a concurrence of school and agency is present with him as he writes long after he has left the agency. His relation to his present situation in school and to his adviser in the writing of the essay has not erased his memory of his agency experience. Throughout his writing of the essay, in his casework class, and in his other classes, his agency is present within him, if not present in fact.

Our experience with essay writing has led us to the realization that this sense of school-agency concurrence which the student carries with him from his field experience has especial relevance and meaning for him when his field adviser becomes his essay adviser. This structure, which enables one faculty person to follow the student from field work experience to essay writing, has prevailed for our students even though other changes in the accustomed advisory structure may need to be made. As our school has grown, it has not always been possible for the casework teacher of the summer to act as field work and essay adviser to all the students of the class, although we believe this to be of optimum value to the student. The alternate plan that we have come to consider sound calls for the case work teacher of both summer and spring terms to be the student's school adviser, as obtains for all students. The alternate plan further calls for another faculty member to be the student's field work and essay adviser.

The adviser who has known the field work agency as

well as the student's experience in it still is not in a position to question the student's words describing the structure of the particular social agency or the nature of its service. He can only question the student's words that do not ring true to his present process and to the learning of the school. In the spring term, the essay adviser needs the agency, and from that need has arisen our practice of sending a draft of the approved essay to the supervisor for criticisms and suggestions about the student's presentation of the agency. After the supervisor's response has been received, the student makes any changes necessary before the essay is typed in its final form.

The supervisors have the difficult duty of reading material that they can change in only a small area and also the disadvantage of reading the essay after eight weeks have elapsed since the student was in the agency. The supervisors, however, have shown a remarkable ability to do this well and with a warm relatedness to the student's creative effort, recognizing that he is now in another process and that the supervisor has not known the living detail of this process. Although there is usually an interchange of correspondence between adviser and supervisor, there is no new experience of concurrence in conference and of course no act of fusion in the sense we have described it in this book. There is, as may be evident, a feeling of concurrence which does continue through the term as both adviser and supervisor are well aware of the agency's necessary place in the campus term.

After several years of having a second meeting of the second-year supervisors on campus at the end of the year, we have instituted it as part of the regular calendar. Such a meeting has seemed to us important for the student in his ending with an agency with which, though he has by now moved quite far from it, he has never really completed his relationship. In this meeting, the adviser and supervisor come together again and conclude the concurrent relationship of the year. The group of supervisors and faculty meet together to discuss some aspects of professional education which might be of interest to all and of particular application to this school and these agencies.

By the end of May, the second-year students are ready for their Commencement in early June and for the jobs they soon shall take. The first-year students having achieved their commencement, and with their placements safely reserved for them in the fall, now peer at the second-year faculty members as if seeing them for the first time as people. The applicants are meeting the initial hint of the two-pronged problem, are being accepted by the school, and are being assigned placements. Another year of the school of social work will soon begin.

8

A RESOLUTION
IN HUMAN RELATIONSHIP

From the functional generative principle and the work in process of the University of North Carolina School of Social Work, its supervisors and students, one resolution of the practice-theory split emerges. As we reflect, in these closing pages, upon the meaning of this resolution, function itself takes on new meaning.

The helping function pervades all those agencies offering help to troubled people and indeed all those individuals who establish themselves as counsellors and therapists. In this sense, the helping function is not the agency function alone, it is a function that originates in man himself through the ages to fulfill a human need to be cared for and to care for those who cannot find their way alone. This need has been met through a helping function carried out by those who chose it, and were charged to do so, in many different and not always helpful ways. It is in this function, however, that the social worker first finds his own life's direction and later integrates into his own wholeness in creative work.

Down through the ages, since before the time of the Good Samaritan, can be seen one clear line of the structuring of this need and desire into formal channels eventually forming the institution of social work. Through the trials and errors of gifts to the poor, through religious organizations, through Poor Laws, through almshouses and workhouses, through charity organizations and family services, settlement houses and child placement agencies, many people have worked to fulfill themselves in this function of helping their fellows in need. Today's social agencies and social service departments in other institutions such as hospitals and prisons are still further outgrowths of this helping function in its becoming the institution, the field, of social work. Although each agency has its own particular function and unique structure, within each agency and each worker must be living this original helping function.

The supervisor who is an employee of one of these social agencies has through the years of his training and experience chosen and become identified with this helping function and with its special manifestation in this one agency. First and foremost, the supervisor's existence as a working person is to help troubled people, particularly those troubled people who sit in his agency's waiting-room.

The teacher, on the other hand, has a very different function. His comes down through the ages out of man's need for knowledge and his satisfying of that need through learning and teaching. Before the days of Socrates students sat at the feet of teachers, and teachers took unto themselves the function of gaining knowledge and of imparting it to others. This need for knowledge and for a function to satisfy it can also be seen finding expression in structures built to accommodate more than the tutor-pupil sessions in the courtyard. The trials and errors, the practice and the theory, of schools and colleges and universities over thousands of years are evidence of man's work to put into action this function of teaching to meet this human need for knowledge and for the process whereby man moves to fulfill his inner potential.

The educational function, too, is a pervasive one extending into every classroom and lecture hall and every tutorial relationship. And with this function the teacher is at all times identified, having chosen it and having been charged to execute it by the school that employs him.

In this way, we see the supervisor and the faculty member who is the student's field work adviser as having separate and distinct functions. Each is a function powerful in its meaning for the individual who possesses it and for the individual who comes to need and to use it. Each function entails the creative work of its practitioners in the course of carrying out the teaching and the helping and also in the development of the function itself. If teachers do no work on perfecting the theory and the practice of teaching, and agency workers do no work on the theory and practice of helping, the professions and the institutions will flounder and perhaps perish. More than that, each function as it is actualized in the teacher's school and the supervisor's agency requires constant work or it too will be rendered impotent. In other words, the teacher has his function and his charge to carry it out and to create within it; the supervisor of an agency charged to help people has his. Their individual and collective strengths as teachers and as helpers lie in the clarity of the differentiation and in the separateness between themselves and between their institutions.

Well that may be, we soon say, but for each of these two particular workers, there are further complexities. We might agree that the supervisor who should be identified with the helping function of his agency is also a teacher when he is in conference with the student. And the school's teacher who is the adviser is also a social worker, for that is the very content he teaches. Rather than adding obstacles to our problem, however, it is here that we may begin to find the solution.

"Concurrence," which has so often been exclusively reserved as a descriptive term for one plan of alternating field and class, has wider meaning. Concurrence means "agreement" as well as "existing at the same time." For teacher and for supervisor, each of whom has a clearly defined basic function, these conditions of concurrence can be met. Even on the Block Plan, the two institutions are coexisting in the interest of the student. On any plan, conferences and meetings can be arranged in which adviser and supervisor are quite aware of their concurrent existence. Agreement may be reached through the administrative pre-placement contract and again through the discussions of supervisor and adviser.

The sense of being contemporary and in agreement might lead to a mutuality in the adviser-supervisor relationship. Mutuality may feel pleasant for both, but the student is unlikely to let mutuality take the place of the single reality; he can easily find a way to slip through to a continuing refusal to release his impulse for growth and his willingness to learn until he meets the real thing.

But concurrence has a further meaning and that is "to meet at a point," and perhaps there is where identity comes about. Meeting at a point, coming to an agreement about the student, each affirming the function that is his own, supervisor and adviser may have arrived at the place where the critical step can be taken. In affirming the function that is his own and not the other's, the supervisor is the present-day representative of the long line of helpers who have preceded him, as is the adviser representative of the long line of teachers. On the supervisor's part this act must be a relinquishing of the teaching function that he has assumed for the special purpose of teaching the casework function and skill, in actual practice of helping his agency's clients. On the adviser's part this act must be a consent to represent the whole of the teaching function wherever it has to do with the university's social work student.

This is an act of concurrence, a meeting at a point with a clear recognition of each other's primary roles. But meeting at a point still leaves a gap between two people, between two separate forces. As long as there is a gap at all, the student will find his way through. In pushing from within, he is seeking truth in his outer world, and only he himself can know it when he finds it in the corresponding reality. Only when he does, can he risk himself finally.

So there must be yet another step. The adviser who represents the teaching function of the student's whole experience includes that of the agency—he could explain this to the student, and the student would sense both the sincerity and yet the insufficiency of his words. The act of fusion which the adviser must perform is an act of will, an integrating within himself of both the teaching function and the helping process, a process that like his own teaching process offers a growth-inducing experience of inner psychic change.

Nothing can transfer the helping function of the agency to the adviser short of his actual employment by the agency. He himself can, however, become so identified with the single process underlying both teaching and helping, and with the educational function that the student is seeking, that he can fuse into his being, for the moment, both school and agency. For the moment, through this act, this hard internal work that needs renewing with each student, he fuses school and agency within him; for the moment he *is* the school-agency, the single reality.

This time, when the student meets his adviser who is the single reality of school and agency, of practice and theory, he chooses. He may refuse; no one can predict his action. What one can say to him is: "At last, here is the single outer reality of your learning which can be yours as your own inner reality, if you will make it so." Here can be the consummation of his inner pressure after truth. If he chooses now to release his life impulse, the potential he has not yet realized, and acts to live and to grow, he has come to the place where inner and outer, practice and theory, become one in human relationship. In that moment when the individual in his inner being feels as truth and takes as his own the other's offering, the outer reality is inner.

Here, then, is the theory to provide the resolution of the duality that the student meets in academic and experiential learning and a solution to his need for singleness in his external reality. We have seen, too, the practice in which one school has attempted to make such singleness available to each of its students.

Are this theory and this practice new? They are new and old and extend the content and experience of the functional generative principle and contribute to it understanding. Whenever some aspect of a generative principle itself is touched, the whole of the functional process is reopened to view. This is the way of generative principles and the work they require for their growth over time. The generative principle holds the new and the old, the past and the present and the future, as long as we work at it. So we come again to the place where we started, to the generative principle, to the historic problem of the practice-theory split, and to the efforts, including our own, to offer the social work student an opportunity to learn, to change, to grow, and to become integrated and whole within himself. There is much work to do. All we have said here of a theory and its imperfect model in practice is but an attempt to take one step toward performing that work.

The age-old puzzle about knowledge and experience, practice and theory, analytic and synthetic, has not been solved in this volume, needless to state. But we do venture to make a suggestion to savant and to practitioner who struggle on, each with his own side of the mystery. This is a human mystery, a human problem, and the place where the outer and the inner can meet is in the course of human relationship. As we said earlier, outer can become inner, theory experience, analytic synthetic, in that moment when an individual in his inner being feels as truth and takes as his own the other's offering, in whatever content or lack of content it may be presented.

If this is the case, and we believe it to be, the future as far as we can see now is unlimited. To look outward at the behavior of others (to observe, to analyze, to tabulate, to graph, to argue about) has its place in the development of a profession of helping and its helpers. To look inward at the behavior of one's own self (at one's thoughts and feelings, one's will and impulses, one's likes and dislikes) has its place, also, in the development of those who choose to become the helpers. To look outward and inward at the same time, even for the fleeting moment, seems to be touching upon transcendence, though we know that in the sense that we have presented this moment here it has been experienced time and again by many, many individuals. Beyond the understanding, however, of philosophy and of psychology it might be; yet this amazing moment when outer and inner meet in the helping relationship holds more power for human growth in professional settings than we have probably begun to suspect. We have far to go.

In concluding this present attempt, this essay, to close the gap of the two-pronged learning situation that the single human student faces, we once again need to mention the life force. For the teacher, the life that he brings to his teaching, this relevance, he makes available for his students. Out of this relevance, he can care for them and for what he teaches—and caring, he can be critical of one in respect to the other. He can admit to the unknown and to the unknowable. He can recognize that inner fears and fondnesses and strengths and irrationalities exist in him and in all mankind as does an inner desire for order and reason. He can cherish for himself and for his students the moments when each can feel the joy of true inner integration when will and emotion and intellect unite in creative work with professional skill and understanding. With him, his students may grow to care for the people they help who come in time of trouble to the social agency, and further to care that their own ability to help will become constantly more effective.